DESIGN IT, SEW IT, AND WEAR IT

DUANE BRADLEY

DESIGN IT, SEW IT, AND WEAR IT

*How To Make Yourself a Super
Wardrobe Without Commercial Patterns*

illustrated by

JUDITH HOFFMAN CORWIN

THOMAS Y. CROWELL   NEW YORK

Library of Congress Cataloging in Publication Data Bradley, Duane.   Design it, sew it, and wear it.
Includes index.
SUMMARY: Gives instructions for designing patterns and combining them to make an
infinite variety of shirts, dresses, skirts, robes, and sweaters.
1. Dressmaking—Juvenile literature. 2. Dressmaking—Pattern design—Juv. lit.
3. Sewing—Juv. lit. [1. Dressmaking—Pattern design. 2. Sewing]
I. Corwin, Judith Hoffman. II. Title.   TT515.B77   646.4   76-55732
ISBN 0-690-01297-7   0-690-03839-9(LB)
1 2 3 4 5 6 7 8 9 10

BY DUANE BRADLEY

Design It, Sew It, and Wear It
How to Make Yourself a Super Wardrobe
Without Commercial Patterns

Sew It and Wear It

Contents

DESIGN IT,
SEW IT,
AND
WEAR IT

· 1 ·

A Top from Rectangles: A Simple Peasant Blouse

Commercial patterns for home sewing were invented during the period of the Civil War; before that time, women who sewed had to make their own. Each seamstress accumulated patterns for various garments, which she adjusted to fit the different members of her family. The body of a shirt, for example, had a certain basic shape, and she learned how to make it longer or shorter or wider or narrower to fit a particular person. There were different kinds of collars, and she had a basic pattern for each and knew how to change its dimensions to fit the wearer. A skilled seamstress who had mastered this method of pattern cutting could see a dress on a friend or in a store window, memorize its distinctive features, return home, and duplicate them for herself. You can learn to do this, too.

A good way to begin is to make a blouse with one of the simplest designs in existence, a top that has been worn for thousands of years by people all over the world.

The drawing shows you how the peasant blouse looks when finished. It's so easy to make that except for the neckline, you won't even need a separate pattern. You can make the blouse in your size by marking the pieces directly on the material itself with a yardstick and a piece of chalk.

The best sort of fabric to use is a poplinlike permanent press, in either a solid color or a print. You may want to make the blouse in a wild print with a sash in a solid color, matching one of the colors in the print, or vice versa. Do not, however, choose a fabric with a design that has an up and down; this blouse is cut in such a way that you would end up with the design upside down on one side of the shirt.

Look at the blouse in the drawing; think about what colors and fabric designs look best on you; and then make up your mind as to what you want to buy. You will need 1¾ yards of 45-inch wide material for the blouse, and ¼ yard of 45-inch wide material for the sash. You will also need approximately ½ yard of ½-inch elastic, and a spool of thread, which should be the same color as the solid-color material. When you stitch a patterned material using thread of one of the colors in the pattern, the thread does not show very much, but if you used bright red thread on a plain yellow material, the stitching obviously would be quite visible.

When you have the material at home, the first thing to do is to make certain that the fabric is perfectly straight. Fold the piece of material in half crosswise with the selvage edges matching on each side. If the raw edges are perfectly straight, you can go right ahead marking your pattern. If they are not, the first thing you must do is to straighten the material. This may sound like a tedious process, but it really isn't difficult, and it is absolutely necessary in order to have a finished garment that fits properly.

To cheer you up in case you do have to straighten the material, it is mastering simple, basic techniques like this—which will become second nature to you in a short time—that makes the difference between a good garment and a poor one. This particular blouse is made of three rectangles of material, plus a sash (which is another rectangle), and a facing for the neckline. If the material is properly cut, the blouse will look like a million dollars on you; if it isn't, the blouse will soon wind up in the Good Will bag, or else embarrass you every time you wear it. Although all the garments in this book are easy to make, they are designed to be the counterparts of expensive, commercially made clothing. Just stick to the rules, and you'll be rewarded with a wardrobe that will delight you.

To straighten material, you need to know something about how it is made. If you look closely at it, you will see that it is woven of two sets of threads— one set running crosswise, the other lengthwise. Follow these threads with your eye, and see if the raw edges are uneven because the material was unevenly cut at the store. If so, trim it properly, following one of the lines of thread with your scissors.

Sometimes the edges are uneven because the mate-

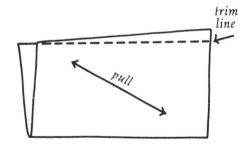

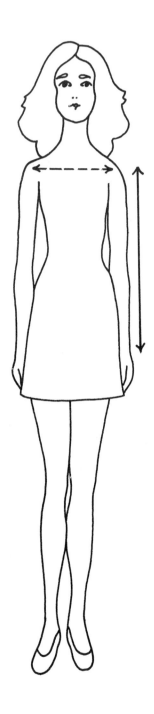

rial was twisted and the threads from which it was woven are out of line. You can usually solve this problem by pulling the material diagonally across the "short" dimension, as shown in the drawing.

If neither method works, pin the selvage edges together evenly and press the material with an iron. If you don't have a steam iron, sprinkle the fabric with water before you press it. Sometimes it is necessary to trim off the selvage edges with scissors and then press the material. If the fabric is still not straight, put it through the washing machine, or launder it by hand, and press it straight while it is slightly damp.

Once your material is properly straight, you are ready to start from scratch and make the blouse to your own measurements. To do this, you need a tape measure, a pencil, a piece of paper, a good cutting surface, a sharp pair of scissors, a yardstick, and a piece of chalk. Regular blackboard chalk is fine, for it is easy to brush off. If you use tailor's chalk, you should do your marking on the wrong side of the cloth, since this chalk is more difficult to erase.

You will need to know the following measurements: the width across your shoulders, the length of your arms, the distance from mid-shoulder to your waistline, and the distance from your waistline to whatever length you wish your blouse to be.

Stand in front of a full-length mirror and locate the tip of your shoulder bone with your fingers. You will feel the edge of the bone toward the back of your shoulder where it joins the arm bone. Locate this point on both shoulders and, with the tape measure, measure across your back. Jot this figure down.

To find your sleeve length, measure from your

shoulder tip (as above) to your wrist bone. Jot this figure down.

To find the distance from mid-shoulder to your waistline, tie a string around your waist at the narrowest part of your body. With the string in place, measure from a point halfway between your shoulder tip and where your neck joins your shoulder to the string around your waist. Jot this figure down.

Measure from your waistline to whatever length you wish the finished blouse to be. The length will depend, of course, on the current style. Sometimes blouses of this sort are worn just below the waistline, and sometimes just above the knees—in which case, they can also be used as short dresses. A standard length for this particular blouse is about 8 inches below the waistline, with another 2½ inches added for the hem. You might use that length as a beginning, when you are chalking the pattern pieces on the cloth, and see how it works out for the amount of material you have and your own particular figure.

Now you are ready to mark the dimensions of your blouse. The width of the body of the blouse is your shoulder measurement plus 9 inches. This includes a ⅝-inch seam allowance and allows for approximately a 4-inch shoulder drop on each side, which will make the blouse wide enough to fit over your hips. The body is to be cut in a single rectangle, front and back together, so that its total length will be the distance from your shoulder to your waist, plus the length you want the blouse to be, plus the hem allowance, times two.

The sleeves are to be made of two identical rectangles 18 inches wide. Their length will be your sleeve length minus 2½ inches. You subtract this

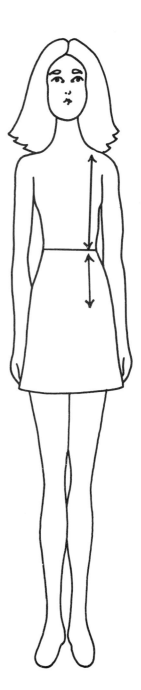

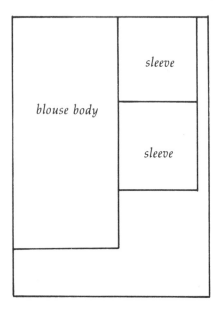

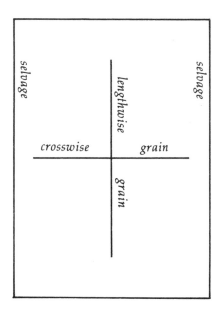

amount because the sleeve line on this blouse falls below the shoulder. The amount includes allowances for seams and hems.

Lay the cloth out flat, and using chalk and a yardstick, draw the three rectangles in these dimensions. The rectangles should be marked on the **straight grain,** which simply means that the edges of the rectangles should be parallel to the straight edge of the fabric. Another way to make sure the rectangles are on the straight grain is to line them up with the long, straight threads in the material.

The rectangles should also be placed on the same grain of the material. Fabrics have two straight grains: a **lengthwise grain** and a **crosswise grain**. Lengthwise is from cut edge to cut edge, and crosswise is from selvage to selvage. Generally speaking, clothes are cut with the lengthwise grain running vertically on the body. If you decide to cut a garment on the crosswise grain—and with many fabrics, you can just as well do this—be sure to cut *all* pieces crosswise. If you forget and put some one way and some another, your garment will not hang properly, and in the case of many prints—stripes, for example—the stripes would run horizontally on some of the pieces and vertically on others. Later on, you may decide you want to cut some decorative elements, such as pockets, in a different direction from the main pattern pieces, but for now, follow the all-one-way rule.

When you are working with a fabric with a design that has a definite up and down—a print with a birdcage design, for instance—you must be careful to place the pattern pieces so that they all face in the same direction on the material. That is, if you were making a blouse in which the front and back were cut separately, both pieces would have to face in the same direction or you would end up with the birdcages upside down on one or the other of the pieces. It is because the body of the peasant blouse is cut all in one piece that you cannot use a print with a definite up and down.

Once you have the rectangles marked on the fabric, you must make a pattern for the **oval neckline** for the peasant blouse, which you will also use to cut a facing for the neckline. Take a piece of scrap material about 15 inches square and fold it in half. Starting at the folded edge, draw a line with chalk across the center of the material to represent the shoulder line of the blouse. Now on the folded edge mark a point 3 inches above and a second point 4 inches below this line. Mark a third point 4 inches out from the fold on the chalked line. Draw a curved line connecting these three points. This results in half of an irregular oval, which is the neckline.

Cut along the lines and unfold the material. Slip the material over your head, with the chalked lines resting on your shoulders and the deeper measurement of the neckline in front. The square should go on easily and lie flat around your neck. If it is too large for you, make another sample neckline, subtracting ½ inch from the position of each of the previous marks. If it is too small, add ½ inch to each. When you have a neckline that pleases you, cut along the original fold line so that you have a pattern for half the neckline only. Trim off the outside edge to a finished width of about 2½ inches. Label it "Oval Neckline," so you'll remember what it is, and mark the front and the back as well as the shoulder line on

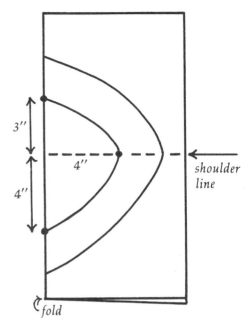

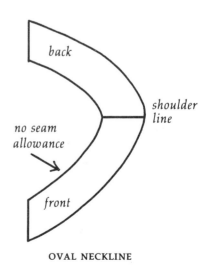

OVAL NECKLINE

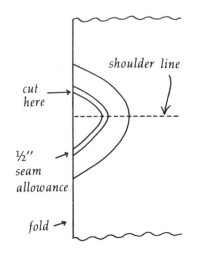

shoulder line

cut here →

½" seam allowance →

fold →

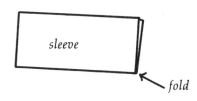

sleeve

← fold

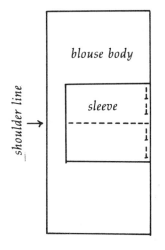

blouse body

shoulder line →

sleeve

it. Mark "no seam allowance" at the neckline edge.

Cut out the body of the blouse first. Fold it in half crosswise at the shoulder line and mark the fold with chalk. Unfold the material and fold it in half lengthwise. Put the neckline pattern on the fold, matching the chalked shoulder lines, and pin it in place. Cut out the oval for the neckline, being sure to add ½-inch seam allowance.

Cut out the sleeves from the material. Fold each sleeve in half lengthwise. Chalk the fold.

Unfold the body of the blouse and both sleeves, and set the sleeves in place, right sides of sleeves to right side of blouse. Match the edges of the sleeves and blouse as shown, and also match the chalked lines so that each sleeve will be centered at the shoulder line. Pin in place with ⅝-inch seams. You are now ready to fit the blouse, and you will see how even a simple garment like this one looks better if it is adjusted to fit your particular body.

When **fitting a garment,** it is usually easiest to put it on inside out. Then once the fit seems right, you can try it on right side out in order to get a more accurate idea of how it will look when it is sewn. Always place the pins with their heads toward your body and the points facing away from it. This will help keep them from sticking you.

To fit the peasant blouse, turn it inside out and pin the side and sleeve seams, making ⅝-inch seams. Begin at the underarm point on each side and continue from there to the end of the sleeve; then pin from the underarm to the bottom of the blouse. Slip on the blouse and look at yourself in the mirror. You can tell better how it will look when finished if you tie a strip of material around your waist to represent the sash.

Look at yourself from the front, from the back, and standing sideways to the mirror. Let your arms hang down naturally at your sides, then move them up and around to see if there is enough ease. After you have done that, you are ready for fine checking.

The shoulder line of the peasant blouse falls down below your natural shoulder line, giving a soft, rounded appearance. If the body of the blouse looks too bulky, it may be that it is too wide for you. If the sleeves look bulky and seem to have too much material, perhaps they need to be made narrower. Repin the side seams or the sleeve seams to make them narrower, then check your appearance in the mirror just as you did before to be sure the new dimensions are right. Notice that this particular kind of sleeve does not have a fitted armhole (which allows for arm movement), so be sure to move your arms up, down, and around to recheck for ease. Don't make the sleeves or the body of the blouse so narrow that the blouse looks fine when are you standing still but will bind you like a strait jacket when you move.

Since the sleeves are to be gathered with elastic at the wrists, you can tie a string around the sleeves now to see how that will change their appearance. This method of checking the dimensions of a garment and fitting it properly before you sew it together takes a little time, but is much easier than sewing the seams first and then having to rip out all those stitches because the fit isn't right.

When you are satisfied with its appearance, take off the blouse and make any necessary changes. Cut away any excess material from the seams, leaving a ⅝-inch seam allowance. In general, when sewing a garment you will make ⅝-inch seams. There are exceptions, such as neckline seams, but they will be indicated as we go along. After that is done, measure the length and width of both body and sleeves, and jot these figures down. The best way to do this is to make a rough sketch of the blouse itself. Label the sketch "Peasant Blouse" and indicate the measurements in their proper places. When you want to make this blouse again, or a variation of it, you will know exactly what the measurements are.

Now you are ready to sew the blouse together. If the side and sleeve seams are still pinned, unpin them to make sewing the sleeves to the blouse easier. You may, if you wish, trim all the raw edges with pinking shears before sewing, as this makes for a neater appearance on the inside of the garment and also reduces raveling. If they are not already in place, pin the sleeves to the blouse as before and sew the two together, making ⅝-inch seams. Now, while the garment is still flat, use your neckline pattern to cut a self-facing for the neckline. This is to be an **inside facing**—that is, it will fall on the inside, not on the outside, of the blouse. Fold a leftover piece of your material in half, lay the pattern on it so that the straight edges are on the fold, pin in place, and cut around the pattern. Be sure to add a ½-inch seam allowance at the neckline edge. The facing should be the same width as the pattern—2½ inches. This will make a neckline facing that exactly fits the neckline itself, so it will be easy to sew in place. While the facing is still separate, turn under and sew a ¼-inch hem all around the outside edge.

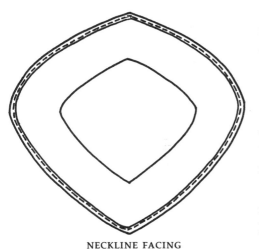

NECKLINE FACING

Lay the body of the blouse out flat and pin the facing in place around the neckline, right side of facing to right side of blouse. Stitch the facing to the neckline with a ½-inch seam.

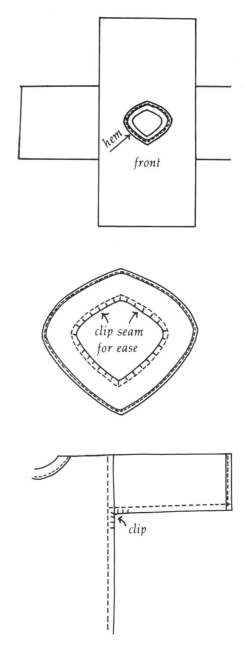

So that the facing will lie completely flat when it is turned to the inside of the blouse, you must **clip the seam for ease.** This is necessary because when the curved edges of two pieces of material are sewn together and then reversed, a strain is put on the material. Use scissors to make short cuts from the outside edge of the seam toward the row of stitches, never cutting through the stitches. Turn the facing to the inside, folding exactly on the seam line, and press it so it lies flat against the blouse. You will finish it later by hand, and are now ready to go on with the rest of the blouse.

Fold the blouse in half, crosswise, wrong side out, and match the side seams, beginning at the underarm point. Pin from this point to the bottom of the blouse and to the ends of the sleeves. Sew the side and sleeve seams with a ⅝-inch seam. Clip into the corners at the underarms to allow the seams to lie flat when the blouse is right side out.

Slip the blouse on, and check the length of the sleeves. As these will be **sleeves gathered with elastic,** you are to finish them with a 1-inch hem to hold the elastic. You can make them any length you like. Fold the end of one sleeve under 1 inch, gather the end of it with your other hand, and push the sleeve up to see how it will look shorter than wrist length. If you want to wear the finished sleeve pushed up above your elbow, you can use a length of elastic that will make it fit snugly there.

Cut the sleeves shorter if you prefer them that way,

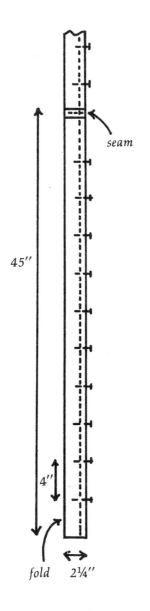

45"

seam

4"

fold   2¼"

and then make the hem on each sleeve. You do this by first folding an inch of the material under, then folding its raw edge under ¼ inch—on the wrong side, of course. Begin stitching on one side of the sleeve seam, and sew around the sleeve until you come to a point ¾ of an inch away from where you started. Leave that much of the hem open, so that you can insert the elastic easily.

Measure around your arm at the point where you want the end of the sleeve to be, add 1 inch, and cut two pieces of elastic this length. Put a safety pin through one end of one of the pieces of elastic and run it through the hem. Lap the ends of the elastic over each other to take up the extra inch you allowed, and stitch together back and forth, either on the sewing machine or by hand. Do the same on the other sleeve. Then sew across the ¾-inch openings you left in the hem of the sleeves.

All the machine sewing on the blouse has now been completed, and you are ready to make the **sash.** Fold the quarter of a yard of material you bought for it in half lengthwise and cut along the fold. This will make two pieces of material, each 4½ inches wide and 45 inches long. Sew the two pieces together, right sides facing, to make one long continuous strip, which will be nearly 90 inches in length. Fold this strip in half lengthwise, inside out, and match the raw edges together, pinning them in place every 4 inches. You are going to sew a seam along this entire length, and when two very long edges of material are sewn together, they tend to slip in the machine. (The top layer pulls more rapidly through the machine than the bottom one.) Pinning the edges securely will

12

help to prevent this. It is also a good idea to check your seam from time to time as you sew. You can tell if it is beginning to pull unevenly. If it is, stop and remove the stitches until you reach the place where the seam runs straight, then resew it. Sew down the length and across one end of the sash, leaving the other end open.

Now you are ready to turn the sash right side out, but first cut off the points of the two corners at the stitched end of the sash as shown in the drawing so that sharp points will be formed when the sash is right side out. Turn the sash right side out by beginning to push the stitched end toward the open end with a pencil. Since this is a wide sash, you will soon find you are able to pull the length of material through very easily. Turn the raw edges at the open end under ½ inch, and sew them together. Iron the sash flat, and it is done.

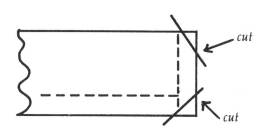

All that remains now is to hand-stitch the hem at the bottom of the blouse and to attach the neckline facing to the blouse. This will be done with "invisible" stitching, a mark of a quality garment. The reason for this is simple—the main seams of a garment can be sewn by machine because they are on the inside and do not show. If you finish hems and attach facings by hand, that stitching won't show either, which is what you want.

Before doing any hand-sewing, it is wise to eliminate the risk of any potential problem caused by knots and snarls in the thread. **Waxing the thread** is one way of preventing such difficulty. You do this by threading the needle and pulling the thread across the edge of a piece of beeswax (sold in notions de-

waxing the thread

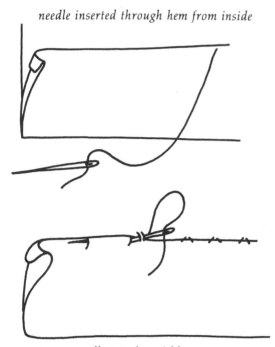

needle inserted through hem from inside

insert needle into hem fold

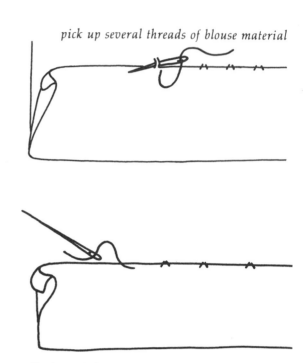

pick up several threads of blouse material

needle through hem fold, ready to insert into blouse

partments) or across the outside of a white candle. Or you can simply hold the thread very tightly between two fingernails and pull it through.

Begin the **invisible stitching** by inserting the needle through the hem of the facing from the inside. This will conceal the knot at the end of the thread. The stitches themselves are very small, and the thread between the stitches is run in between layers of material so that it does not show when the work is done. Take a very small stitch through the material of the blouse itself, picking up only two or three threads, then insert the needle into the hem fold and slide it along for a half inch. Bring the needle up through the hem fold close to the edge, pick up two or three threads on the blouse as before, then again insert the needle into the fold, and continue in this way around the entire facing.

When the facing is finished, fold the 2½-inch bottom hem in place, and turn the raw edge inside ¼ inch. It is a big help to iron the folded hem in place, and quite a lot easier than pinning it along its entire length. Sew the hem with invisible stitches in the same way you did the facing. This is a **standard hem.**

Press the blouse when you are finished, and try it on. Wrap the sash twice around your waist and tie a knot to hold it. Look at yourself in the mirror and see what a beautiful garment you have made! It wasn't really very difficult this time, and every time you make a similar blouse it will be easier. This particular pattern looks well in various fabrics, and you can change its appearance completely by using different fabrics and decorative trims.

In the course of making this one simple blouse, you have learned a number of basic techniques, including how to take your own measurements, to cut a pattern for an oval neckline, to design a particular style of garment to fit yourself, to straighten material, to make an inside facing, to make a sash, and to use invisible stitching.

In the next chapter you will learn to use this basic style to make two other garments that are so unlike in appearance no one would ever guess that all three came from the same source.

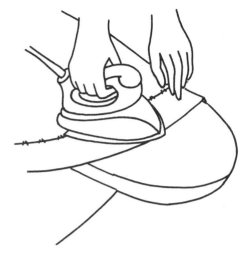

· 2 ·

Two More Simple Tops: A Country Shirt and a Happi Coat

COUNTRY SHIRT

The country shirt is a casual, colorful overblouse that is made in the same basic way as the peasant blouse. The best fabric for it is unbleached muslin, which looks very much like the plain homespun cotton from which real peasant clothes were made. Before purchasing the material, you need to make a pattern, so you can estimate how much cloth to buy. Although the country shirt is very much like the peasant blouse, there are differences that will change the amount of material required. Also, unbleached muslin comes in a variety of weights and widths, and you may find a kind you like that is 36 inches wide instead of the 45-inch width you used for the peasant blouse.

Estimating the amount of material is an important part of sewing, because it enables you to meet two

16

common needs. The first is to know *exactly* how much material you require to make a particular garment; the second is to be able to know what garment or garments can be made from a given piece of material. As to the first, you will always have some scraps of material left over after you have cut out a garment, and these scraps will often come in handy for trimming other garments, but it is extravagant to buy a great deal more fabric than you immediately need. When you are planning to use an expensive material, knowing how to estimate accurately the amount you need will save you considerable money. As to the second, you will often come across remnants or odd lengths of material that you like very much, but for which you have no present plan. If you see a piece of wool that would make a handsome skirt, for example, you need to know instantly whether there is enough material to make a skirt for you. If you come across a length of print that would make an attractive blouse, you need to know just how much material you need. When you have become practiced in estimating material, you will be able to take advantage of such bargains without fear of wasting your money.

There are two ways of estimating the amount of material needed for a particular project, either one of which may prove best for you. The first is to cut the actual pattern pieces and then to sketch the dimensions of suitable fabric with chalk on a wooden or linoleum floor. (Chalk marks can be easily removed from these surfaces.) The standard width today of most dress fabrics is 45 inches; of upholstery material, fake fur, and woolens, 60 inches. Unbleached muslin and some special fabrics come in various other

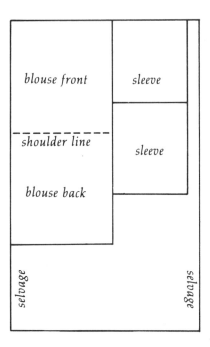

widths. If the material you plan to use comes in only one width, draw a rectangle that wide and 2 yards long on the floor, and lay out the pattern pieces on it. Remember you will want to have all the pieces placed on either the lengthwise or crosswise of the material (see Chapter 1), so move them around until you have found an arrangement that makes the most economical use of fabric. You may find you need to re-sketch the dimensions in order to use the fabric folded; or of course, you may need more yardage.

If the material you plan to use comes in various widths, experiment with each of them until you know which arrangement of pattern pieces on which width will be most economical. It's a good idea to sketch the final arrangement on a piece of paper, so you will be able to reproduce it on the actual fabric.

The second method of estimating material is to tape sheets of newspaper together to duplicate the various widths of fabric. After the paper has been prepared, use it exactly as you used the sketched dimensions on the floor. In this case, you can draw around the pattern pieces with a crayon or felt-tip marker, and use this sketch later as a guide when cutting the actual garment.

Before you can estimate the amount of unbleached muslin you will need for the country shirt, you must know **how to make a pattern** for it. Some of the patterns in the book can be cut from newspaper, but for the most part it is best to make them from cloth. Since newspaper is stiff and will not drape like fabric, it should be used only for patterns that do not need to be fitted to the body, such as pockets and collars, or when nothing else is available. Cloth should be used for the main parts of patterns for shirts and blouses, skirts, dresses, and so forth, as well as for some sleeves and necklines. The patterns should be made of cloth that has enough body to hold its shape and is easy to use. A discarded sheet is excellent, as are muslin and other large pieces of fabric that are not too stiff.

Once you have made a pattern that fits you perfectly, you will want to make it part of a permanent collection. Almost every pattern in this book can be used over and over, sometimes to make duplicate garments in different fabrics or colors, and sometimes to make garments that are quite unlike the original ones. With finished cloth patterns that you know you will often use, you may want to stiffen them. This is not really necessary, but it will make them easier to handle. If the pattern material you use is suitable, you can simply starch the finished version very heavily, iron it, mark it properly, and put it in your collection. If the pattern material cannot be starched without shrinking, you can buy a length of inexpensive material, wash it, cut the final pattern from it, and starch it heavily as before. You might find an already stiffened fabric on sale, such as buckram or an interlining material; in this event, you would not need to starch the pattern. Another method is to buy a large amount of heavy brown kraft paper, such as is used to wrap meat or postal packages, and cut your final pattern from it.

To cut the pattern for the country shirt, refer to the measurements you jotted down for the peasant blouse in Chapter 1. From your pattern-cutting material, cut three rectangles of the proper dimensions for

2″

2½″

2½″

4″

shoulder line

15″

the body of the shirt and the two sleeves. Fold the rectangle for the body in half crosswise and chalk along the fold. This will be the shoulder line.

The main differences between the country shirt and the peasant blouse are that the neckline and body of the former are more fitted; the sleeves are shorter and narrower; and the collar is a short stand-up one.

Before fitting the pattern, you need to make a pattern for the new neckline, which will be a simple **fitted neckline.** (This pattern will be used to cut the neckline facing as well, and should become part of your permanent collection since it will be used many times in the future.) Take a piece of scrap material about 15 inches square and fold it in half. Unfold it and fold it in half the other way. One fold marks the center front and back of the pattern; the other, the shoulder line. Mark each fold with chalk. Where the two chalk lines cross in the center of the material is the center point of the neckline opening. Fold the material in half.

On the fold, with a piece of chalk, mark one point 2 inches above the center point of the neckline and a second point 2½ inches below it. Mark a third point on the shoulder line 2½ inches from the center point. Draw a curved line to connect these three points. With scissors, cut along the curved line, through both thicknesses of material, and you have a neckline opening. Since, however, it is not large enough to go over your head, you need to add a front opening. Mark a point 4 inches down from the bottom of the neckline opening on the center front line. Cut this distance down the fold.

Slip the pattern over your head and look at yourself in the mirror. If the neckline is too large, it will not fit snugly around the base of your neck, and if it is too small, it will pull out of shape. If it is too small, turn your head from side to side to make creases in the material around the inside edge of the neckline, which will show you where to mark changes in the neckline with chalk. If it is too large, try pinning small tucks in the neckline until it fits. Your aim is to create a neckline pattern that will fit smoothly and easily, with no bulges or strains. Do not leave a seam allowance, as that would make it harder to get a good fit. Take the pattern off, make the changes, then try it on again. If you ruin the first pattern, begin over again and keep making changes until you are satisfied.

When the fit of the neckline pleases you, take off the pattern and cut all around the outside of the neckline and front opening 2½ inches from the edge. This is your fitted neckline pattern, and also the pattern for the facing. Label the pattern "Fitted Neckline," mark the shoulder line on it, and add "no seam allowances."

Fold the shirt pattern in half lengthwise, then fold the neckline pattern in half along the center front and back lines. Pin the neckline pattern on the shirt pattern, matching the shoulder lines, adding a ½-inch seam allowance, and cut the front slit opening. Remove the pattern.

Pin the sleeves in place just as you did on the peasant blouse, but do not pin the sleeve and side seams together yet. Now you are ready to fit the pattern.

Turn it inside out as you did the peasant blouse. Pin the pattern together at the underarm point on each side and fold the ends of the sleeves under to see how different sleeve lengths look on you. A typical

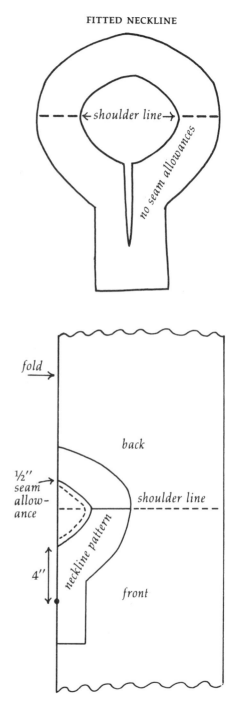

FITTED NECKLINE

← shoulder line →

no seam allowances

fold →

back

½" seam allow- ance

shoulder line

neckline pattern

4"

front

length for the sleeve of the country shirt is 3 inches below the elbow, but you can make yours either longer or shorter.

Pin the sleeve seam to make a narrower sleeve than on the peasant blouse. The sleeve should not be too tight, so you might begin by pinning a new width that is 3 inches wider than your arm. (Pinch the material together so it fits tightly around your arm, then move your fingers outward 1½ inches. Since the sleeve is doubled, pinning it here will give you a sleeve 3 inches wider than your arm at this point. Pin from the end of the sleeve to the seam line where the sleeve joins the body of the shirt.

Beginning at your bust line, pin the side seams to make the shirt narrower. Using the same technique as with the sleeves, hold the back and front of the shirt together on each side at the bust line so that it fits tightly. Move your hand outward on each side 1½ inches, and pin at that spot. Continue this down both sides of the shirt so that you have 3 inches of ease on each side. As you pin, be sure that both side seams are identical.

Now check the length of the shirt. A typical length is 8 or 9 inches below the waistline. Fold the bottom edge of the shirt under at different lengths to see which is more becoming to you. (If the pattern itself is too short to make the shirt as long as you would like it, jot down the amount of material that will have to be added to make it the right length.)

You now have a beginning pattern with changes marked by a lot of pins that are apt to stick you as you take it off. Before removing it, take out all the pins on one side, in both the sleeve and the body. If you have pinned properly, both sides are exactly the same, so the side with the pinned seams will serve as a pattern for the unpinned one.

With the pattern folded at the shoulder line, place it on a flat surface, such as the floor or a table, the pinned side out, and cut off a sleeve end to whatever length you want the sleeves to be. You pinned the sleeve up to the seam where the sleeve is joined to the body and pinned the side from the bust line down, leaving the seam in the area of the underarm unpinned. With chalk, make a curved line to connect the sleeve and side seam. Trim the rest of the sleeve seam and the side seam to 1½ inches from the pins. (This allows some margin for any corrections you need to make at the time of the final fitting.)

Fold the shirt pattern in half again, with the fold on the center line, and trim the other sleeve and side to match the first. If the shirt pattern was longer than you wished, cut it to the proper length. If it was too short, pin a strip of material on both back and front to lengthen it.

All outside edges of this shirt are to be finished with a bound edge, so you do not need to add any hem allowance to the length of the sleeves or the bottom of the shirt itself.

Baste together the new side and sleeve seams and remove all pins. Now that the pattern fits the body more closely, it is better to baste than to pin, since a basted seam is more flexible—and it also doesn't prick! Try the pattern on once again with the basted seams on the outside, so it will be easy to alter them if necessary. Look at yourself very carefully in the mirror—from the front and from each side, and arrange a second mirror so you can get a good view of your back. Pin any changes you wish to make in the

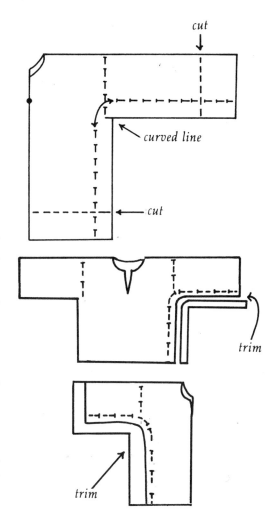

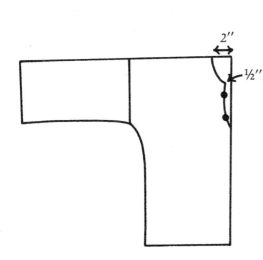

side seams, but always check the changes by moving your arms up, down, and around, bending your body in different directions. The finished shirt should not be so tight that it will bind you when you move.

When you turn sideways to the mirror, be sure the side seams make a straight line down your sides, and those of the sleeve make a straight line down your underarms. Notice also whether the shirt bulges in front or in back—this can be caused by too snug a fit around the hips or too much width at the waistline. Although this shirt is not intended to fit tightly, you may find it looks better if you curve the side seams slightly inward at the waistline.

Be sure to check the length again. A short top generally makes the figure look shorter; a long one makes it look taller. A top that ends exactly at the widest part of the figure makes it look wider. You can get a much better idea of the proper length of the shirt now that the side seams have been basted in place.

Before taking off the pattern, locate the exact positions of waistline and hip line and mark them on the pattern. (You can find your hip line in the same way you found your waistline—by tying a string around it; the hip line is the widest part of the body below the waist.) Remove the pattern and make any changes indicated by this last fitting, leaving a ⅝-inch seam allowance for all seams.

You are now ready to complete the finished pattern. Fold it in half lengthwise, and be sure the neckline area is perfectly flat. Mark a point ½ inch out and 1 inch up from the bottom of the neckline slit, and another point ½ inch out and 1 inch down from the top of the neckline slit. Draw a curved line from the bottom of the neckline slit through each of these

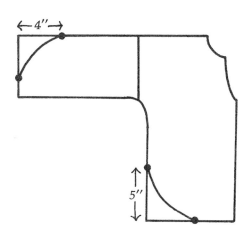

points up to the neckline to make a slot opening.

Now you are going to make curved edges on both sides of the bottom of the shirt and on one side of the ends of each sleeve. On one side seam, mark a point 5 inches from the bottom of the blouse. On the bottom of the shirt, mark a point 5 inches from the side seam. Draw a curve between these two points as shown. Repeat on the other side. Draw a similar curve on the end of each sleeve, only make the points 4 inches from the corner. Cut along the curves.

This part of the pattern is now completed, so label the body "Country Shirt" and each sleeve "Country Shirt, sleeve." Mark "no hem allowance" at the bottom of the shirt and the ends of the sleeves, "½-inch seam allowance" at the neckline, and "⅝-inch seam allowance" on all other seams.

The pattern for the stand-up collar is very simple; it is a strip 4 inches wide and the length of the inside of the neckline, plus 1 inch. You really do not need to cut a pattern for it, but do remember to include it when estimating the amount of material you need.

You will also need bias binding to finish the bottom edge of the shirt and sleeves. To find out how much you require, measure the bottom edge of the front of the shirt and the circumference of one sleeve, and multiply these amounts by two. You can buy this much prefolded commercial bias binding, or you can make your own, whichever you prefer; but learning to make your own bias binding quickly and easily is such a handy technique to master that the latter is recommended. To make 8 feet of 1-inch-wide bias binding, a piece of material 1 foot square is required. If you haven't enough material of the right color left over from a previous sewing project, you can look on

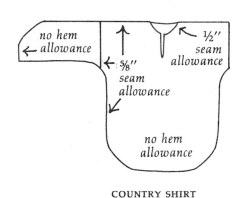

COUNTRY SHIRT

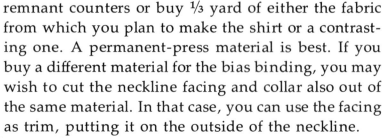

remnant counters or buy ⅓ yard of either the fabric from which you plan to make the shirt or a contrasting one. A permanent-press material is best. If you buy a different material for the bias binding, you may wish to cut the neckline facing and collar also out of the same material. In that case, you can use the facing as trim, putting it on the outside of the neckline.

Use your pattern pieces now to estimate the amount of material you need. Do not forget the collar, the neckline facing, and the bias binding. Before buying the material, however, you should think about how you want to trim the blouse, as the colors you choose for the trim should blend with the color you select for the bias binding. Country shirts of this type are often decorated with a floral design, which you can add by embroidery, by appliqué, or by drawing directly on the shirt with permanent felt-tip markers. Hand-decorated garments, whatever the method used, are always much more expensive than plain ones, and learning to design and produce your own decorations is a lot of fun.

Here are a few ideas to start you off; you can look at fashion magazines for further inspiration. Using tracing paper, you can trace a floral design from a magazine or book or newspaper and then transfer the design to your shirt with dressmaker's carbon paper. Since many effective designs are quite simple, you might sketch one directly on the shirt. Use a soft pencil for sketching, and later cover the pencil marks with felt-tip marker or embroidery, so that the marks don't show. You can cut simple flower shapes from scraps of colored material and appliqué them to the shirt. In doing this, cut the shapes ¼ inch larger

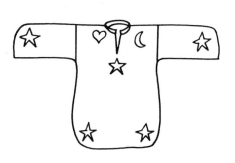

than the finished flower will be, then cut tiny slits ¼ inch deep in the edge of the shape so you can turn the edge under evenly. Baste the shapes in place, turning the edges inside, and sew them down by hand with invisible stitching or with an embroidery stitch.

You should decide on the decoration before buying the material, as the colors you choose for it should blend with the color you select for the bias binding. Besides the unbleached muslin for the shirt, the material for the bias binding, and the equipment for the decoration, you will also need a spool of thread that matches the muslin and one that matches the bias binding. Ordinary white thread will do for the shirt, but off-white is better.

If you are **making your own bias binding,** you can use one of two methods. We think that once you've mastered the second, you will use it the rest of your life.

Bias binding is a strip of material cut diagonally to the weave of the cloth. It is used for facing and for binding the raw edges of seams. It can be made by folding a square of material into a triangle, being sure the fold is on a precise diagonal, and then cutting the folded triangle into strips, each an inch wide. The strips are cut parallel to the fold. These strips must be sewn together on the diagonal in order to preserve the stretch of the material, which is the quality that makes bias binding so useful. To do this, the ends of the strips must be laid together so that the diagonal threads of one end match the diagonal threads of the other—the proper position is shown in the drawing. If you make a mistake and stitch an end of material with the threads straight to an end of

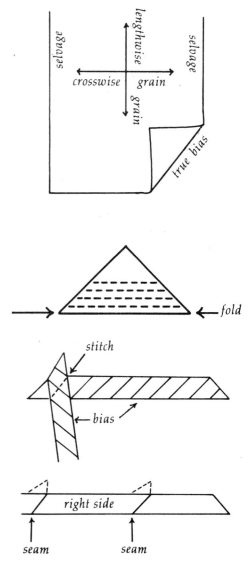

material with the threads diagonal, you nullify the stretch at that point, and the binding will not fit smoothly.

That is one way of making bias binding, but here's the professional way (if the directions puzzle you when you first read them, simply take a paper napkin and cut and baste it according to the directions, and you will see that the procedure is really very simple):

Cut a square of material with 12-inch-long sides. Fold the square in half diagonally, making a triangle. Cut along the fold. Put the two triangles down flat to make what looks like a slanted rectangular shape, then, as shown, mark the side edges with chalk. (This is so you will be able to recognize them after the next step is taken.) Place one triangle back over the other, right side of material to right side of material, so that edges AB and CD are ready to be sewn together in a seam. Offset the edges ¼ inch as shown. Sew the edges together, making a ¼-inch seam. Press the seam open.

At this point it is a help to mark off the strips that you will cut. Beginning at one diagonal edge, on the *wrong* side of the material, draw parallel lines 1¼ inches apart across the entire piece.

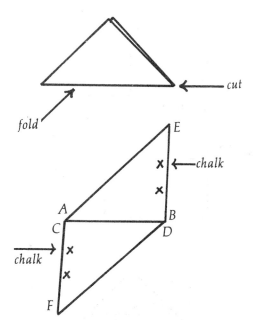

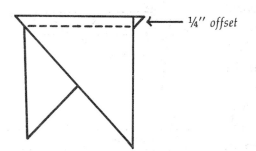

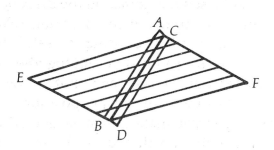

Now locate those two edges you marked with chalk and put them together, right side of material to right side of material. To do this you will have to fold the fabric into a short, fat tube. Bring corner E down to corner AC, and corner F up to corner BD, and you will have formed the tube. Offset the edges 1¼ inches as shown, and pin a ¼-inch seam. This may seem difficult, but just takes a bit of adjusting. Check to be sure that after pinning, the diagonal lines match across the seam; then sew the seam. You will be intersecting with the first seam at both ends of this one.

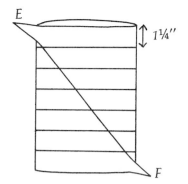

When the second seam is sewn, you have a short wide tube of material on the bias. Following the diagonal lines, begin cutting a strip 1¼-inch wide at one end of the tube and continue until you have cut all of the tube into one long continuous strip of bias binding. It should be about 8 feet long, which will probably be enough to bind all the necessary edges of the country shirt.

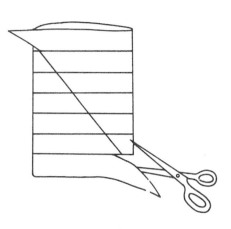

For other projects, if you offset the edges a different amount, you can cut different widths of bias binding. The amount of the offset should be the width of the binding you want plus ¼ inch for the seam.

You are now almost ready to cut out the shirt, but because unbleached muslin shrinks, you must wash the fabric before you use it. Even if the muslin shrinks only 1 inch per yard, that much would make a big difference in the appearance of the finished garment. One way to shrink unbleached muslin is to put it through the normal laundry process, but a second way is to put it into a basin, saturate it with boiling water, and then rinse it in cold water. Press the material after it is dry, and it is ready for use.

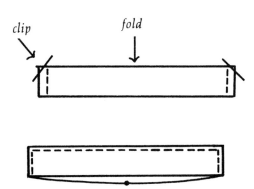

clip   fold

To cut out your material, you will need a sharp pair of scissors, a large flat surface on which to work—the floor is fine—and something to hold the pattern pieces in place as you cut. You can pin the pattern pieces to the material, if you like, but some people find it is easier to hold them down with knives and forks and spoons.

Following the layout you used when estimating material, place all the pattern pieces so that they run the same way on the fabric. Cut the neckline collar and facing from either the shirt material or the trimming material, whichever you decided to use.

A cardinal rule of dressmaking is always to do as much work as possible while a garment is still flat, and before the side seams, which make it into a tube, have been sewn. With this shirt, you can do most of the finishing steps first.

Begin by attaching the **stand-up collar** and the neckline facing. Measure the inside of the neckline of the shirt, up to the slot opening on each side, and add one inch. Cut a strip of material that long and 4 inches wide. Fold this collar strip in half lengthwise, and sew a ½-inch seam across each end. Clip the corners at the folded edge. Turn the collar right side out, pulling the corners you clipped out to a point (you clipped them to remove excess material so this could be done), and sew around the entire outside edge, ¼ inch from the fold.

Fold the collar in half, crosswise, to locate the center point. Fold the shirt neckline in half to locate the center point of the back of the neckline. Mark each center point with a pin.

On the neckline facing, duplicate the slot opening

you cut in the shirt front. Then fold the facing in half to locate the center of the back of the neckline, mark that point with a pin, and prepare to make a sandwich of shirt, collar, and facing.

To make a shirt with an **outside facing,** turn the shirt wrong side out, put the collar around the neckline and pin it in place, matching the center backs by the pins in each. Set these pins about an inch from the raw edge. Now place the neckline facing over this, right side down against the collar. Again match the center back exactly, and line up the facing with the slot opening. Pin all three layers together. Put these pins nearer the raw edges, and remove those that held the collar in place. Use enough pins to hold everything firmly.

Sew the sandwich together with a ½-inch seam, stitching around the inside of the neckline first, then around the slot opening in front. Your seam can be narrower around the slot opening; a ¼-inch seam is enough here. Remove the shirt from the machine and clip any projecting points in the seam. Clip, also, to ease the curved areas (see Chapter 1). After this is done, turn the shirt right side out, and fold the neckline facing in place on the outside of the shirt. The collar will stand up. Be sure that the facing lies perfectly flat. Turn the raw edges of the facing under and stitch in place. If you wish to make the shirt with an inside facing, follow the same directions exactly, except begin by turning the shirt right side out, and make your sandwich with the collar in the middle and the facing on top as before. When you fold the facing, it will be on the inside of the shirt, and the collar will stand up.

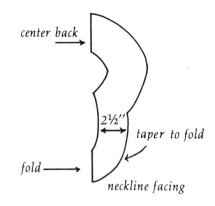

center back

2½″

taper to fold

fold

neckline facing

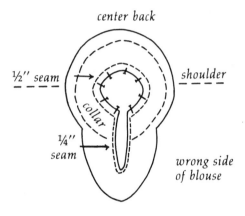

center back

½″ seam

¼″ seam

collar

shoulder

wrong side of blouse

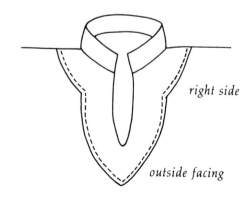

right side

outside facing

31

binding,
right side down

wrong side of shirt

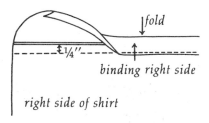

↓fold

$1\frac{1}{4}''$

binding right side

right side of shirt

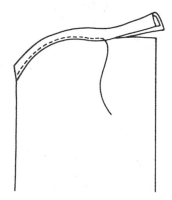

Sew the sleeves to the shirt just as you pinned them, but leave the sleeve seams and the side seams of the shirt open.

You are now ready to **apply the bias binding** on the ends of the sleeves and the bottom of the shirt. Cut a piece of bias binding the length of the end of one sleeve, and pin it in place, beginning at what will be the underarm seam. Put right side of binding to wrong side of shirt, matching the raw edges exactly, and sew in place with a ¼-inch seam. Fold the binding along the seam line and turn to the right side of the shirt. Fold the raw edge under so that the binding just covers the first row of stitches, and pin it in place. Stitch down. On this shirt, machine stitching will be fine, but some time you may wish to use the pattern to make a dressier shirt. Then you should sew this edge down with invisible stitches (page 14) to make a nicer finish.

If you use prefolded commercial bias binding, you can of course just pin it in place over the raw edge, and sew it down with one seam. Be sure to have the shorter edge of the folded tape on the front, so that your stitches will catch the wider edge on the underneath side.

Apply the binding to the other sleeve end and to the bottom back and front of the shirt in the same way.

You may want to add any decorations to the shirt at this point, instead of waiting until the side seams are sewn.

Once the decorations have been completed, turn the shirt wrong side out, match the underarm seams on both sides, and pin from there to the end of the sleeve on each side and to the bottom of the shirt

on each side. Sew the sleeve and side seams, using a
⅝-inch seam. With your scissors, clip the underarm
seams just as you clipped the inside seams at the
neckline, to create ease in those seams.

HAPPI COAT

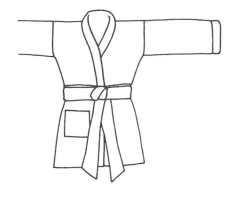

Another garment made from rectangles is the Happi
coat. Really short kimonos, Happi coats were
formerly worn by workmen in Japan. (Happi is a
Japanese word, which, incidentally, does not mean
happy.) The coat is made basically in the same way as
the peasant blouse in Chapter 1, but it has a front
opening and a different neckline. It also has a
wider sash. The coat can be any length you wish, but
a becoming length is that of a tunic blouse—about 8
inches below the waistline. Using the measurements
for the peasant blouse, making any changes in length
you wish, figure the necessary yardage for the coat.
Be sure to allow for a 2-inch hem, front and back, when
you are figuring the length.

The trimming of the Happi coat is a wide binding
around the ends of the sleeves, around the neckline,
and down both sides of the front opening, and the
wide sash. This binding is not cut on the bias. It is
cut 4 inches wide and crosswise of the cloth, as is the
sash, which is 8 inches wide. A yard of 45-inch material will probably be enough to make both the binding and the sash. Here is the way this figure is esti-
mated. A yard of material is 36 inches long, and 4
will go into 36 nine times. Three 4-inch strips of material will use 12 of the 36 inches of 45-inch material,
and make a total of 135 inches of binding, which
should be enough to bind the front opening of the

tunic-length Happi coat. Twelve inches is one third of a yard. The remaining two thirds, or 24 inches, will make 3 strips of material 8 inches wide, which will make a sash 135 inches long.

You will need to reestimate the amount of material you need if your coat is not going to be tunic length. After you have cut out your pattern, you can measure around the end of each sleeve, around the neckline, and down both sides of the front opening, and see if 135 inches of binding will be enough to finish them. You can wrap a string twice around your waist and tie it in a bow or knot, making the ends whatever length you wish, then take it off and measure the string to see if it is more or less than 135 inches long. Fabric can be bought in whatever length you wish, so if you need more for either binding or sash, add the appropriate amount to the original yardage.

You do not have to cut a complete pattern for the Happi coat, but you will need one for the neckline and front opening. To make it, sketch a rectangle on newspaper the size of the front of the peasant blouse. (The size of the front would of course be one half the length of and the same width as the original rectangle.) Fold the rectangle in half lengthwise and mark a point on the center fold 14 inches from the top. Mark another point on the shoulder line 2½ inches out from the center fold. Use a yardstick to make a slanted line connecting these two points. Cut along this line to make a **kimono neckline,** then continue cutting down the center fold to open the pattern down the front. Use one of the halves as your pattern, and mark it "Happi Coat, front neckline."

The Happi coat and the trimming should be made of the same permanent-press material, either a poplin

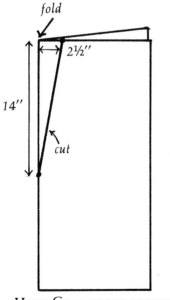

HAPPI COAT, FRONT NECKLINE

type or a plissé, and the trimming should be a different pattern or color. The coat might be a solid color, and the trim flowered, or vice versa, or you may want to use two contrasting solid colors. As with the peasant blouse, do not buy a fabric that has a design running up and down. You will need a spool of thread to match the color of each material. The top stitching on the binding will look better if it matches the binding exactly.

Use the dimensions of the peasant blouse (with any changes you have decided to make in the length) to cut out the parts of the Happi coat from the material. Cut the main body and the two sleeves. Fold the body in half crosswise at the shoulders, mark the shoulder line, and use the new pattern to cut the front neckline and opening. Put the body of the garment on, cross the right front side over the left, and look at yourself in the mirror. Check your appearance from the back to see whether you need to cut a shallow curve at the back of the neckline to make the coat fit better. Remember that the entire neckline will be finished with a 1½-inch binding, and see if you need to make the neckline itself a bit wider. (When making changes of this sort, always cut very carefully, taking off only a small bit at a time, and then try on the garment again. It is quite easy to cut off too much if you don't check the results frequently and fairly tedious to try to replace material you have cut away.)

Before you do any sewing, pin the Happi coat together just as you did the peasant blouse and the country shirt. Center the sleeves, then sew them to the body, but leave the sleeve and side seams open.

The trimming for the body of the coat is sewn on while the garment is still flat. It is a **kimono binding**

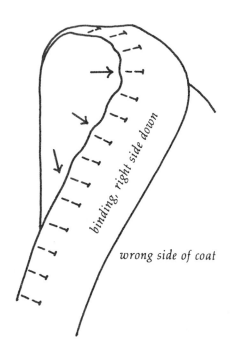

binding, right side down

wrong side of coat

and is put on differently from conventional bindings. It represents another solution to the problem of binding a curved edge.

Sew together enough 4-inch-wide strips of material to make the binding for this part of the garment, and pin it along the front opening of the coat, *right* side of binding to *wrong* side of coat, beginning at the bottom on one side of the front opening.

Match the raw edges exactly and continue pinning the binding in place around the neckline and down the other side of the front opening. When you are pinning around the neckline, you may decide that the job simply can't be done, but all it requires is a bit of care. When you put bias binding around a curved edge, the angle on which the binding was cut allows it to fit smoothly into place. You are now putting a straight binding around a curved edge, and the edge and the binding must be eased together to fit smoothly. Keep that fact in mind as you work, and don't pin the binding either too loose or too tight.

After you have finished pinning, sew the binding in place with a ½-inch seam. Fold it back over the front of the coat, and see if it is really smooth and even. If it isn't, you will be able to see immediately where the trouble is. Just pull out the stitches that are wrong and try again. Even if you have to rip out the stitches and sew on the binding several times, it is worth the effort, for you are learning a technique you will use over and over again.

Once you have the binding properly placed, fold it back over the front of the material and turn the remaining raw edge under, just over the first row of stitches. Get out your iron and ironing board and

36

press the binding in place, then pin it. Taking pains at this point will make finishing the binding a breeze. When you are done pinning, sew it down on top of the first row of stitches. You can do the sewing either on the machine or by hand, using invisible stitches (see page 14).

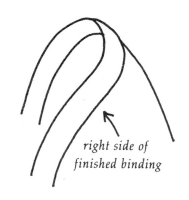

*right side of
finished binding*

Try on the Happi coat again and check the length of the sleeves. They will be 1½ inches longer when the binding is added, so you may want to cut them a bit shorter now.

The binding is to be put on the ends of the sleeves just as it was put around the edge of the neckline and front opening, but you will find it is far easier to apply it to the sleeves because you are now putting a straight binding on a straight edge. Cut 4-inch wide strips of binding the same length as the sleeve ends. With the sleeves still flat, pin the binding in place, right side of binding to wrong side of sleeve. Sew this first seam, and then press the binding out flat away from the sleeve. Before finishing the binding, sew the side seams and sleeve seams together as you did on the peasant blouse, beginning at the underarm seam and sewing to the ends of the sleeves and the bottom of the blouse. Your seam will continue to the end of the binding. Now you are ready to finish the binding—just fold it over and sew it down as before.

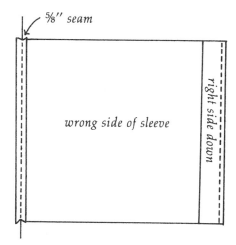

⅝″ seam

wrong side of sleeve

right side down

The sash is made exactly the way the sash in Chapter 1 was made, using material 8 inches wide.

The Happi coat is now finished, except for the 2-inch bottom hem, which is to be a standard hem sewn just like the one on the peasant blouse. Hang the coat on a hanger and suspend it in a doorway to fold up and pin the hem, remembering to turn the

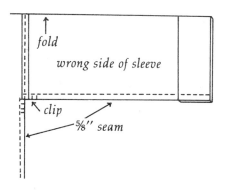

fold

wrong side of sleeve

clip

⅝″ seam

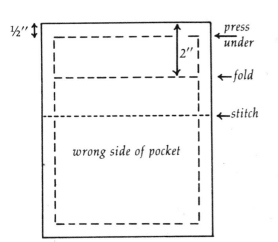

½″ ↕

2″

press under

←*fold*

←*stitch*

wrong side of pocket

raw edge inside ¼ inch. Be careful to match the hem at each side of the front opening and at each side seam to be sure it is even all around the bottom of the coat. Press it in place after it has been folded, then sew.

Put the Happi coat on, wrap the sash twice around your waist and tie it with a knot, then admire yourself in a mirror. If the sight makes you want to run right out to buy some more material to make another coat, try one in terry cloth this time, and wear it over your bathing suit at the beach.

If you would like a **patch pocket** on either of these garments, that's very easy to accomplish. Your pocket can be square or rectangular, and any size you wish. You can use material that matches either the garment or the trim, or contrasts with them, and you will need a piece 1 inch wider and 2½ inches longer than the desired size of the finished pocket. Fold a 2-inch hem at the top of the pocket, turn under the raw edge ½ inch, press, and stitch. Press a ½-inch single hem around the other three sides of the pocket. *Put on the garment and pin the pocket in the place that is most convenient for you.* (This is important, because if you pin a pocket on a garment you are not wearing, and sew it in place, it is not nearly so apt to suit you as if you pin it when you have the garment on.) Before stitching, be sure the pocket is absolutely straight with the weave of the material and the lines of the garment. Unpin the pocket, if need be, and line up the pocket bottom with the bottom of the garment, and the pocket sides with the side seams of the garment. Repin the pocket carefully and then stitch in place as shown, backstitching two or three times at the top on each side of the pocket for security. This is called a patch pocket because it is put on like a patch, and you will be making lots of them before you are through.

These first three garments are all what is known as "easy-fit," or nontailored. In the next chapter you will discover how to make a blouse that fits much more closely, so have your scissors ready!

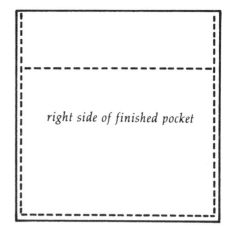

right side of finished pocket

· 3 ·

A Closer Fit:
A Basic Blouse
and a Tennis Shirt

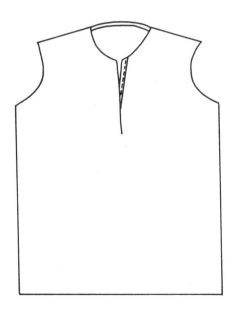

The single most important thing about a garment is that it should fit where it is supposed to fit. You would look better in a burlap bag that was the right size for you than in a satin evening gown of the wrong dimensions. The blouses in the first two chapters were not intended to fit the body closely at any point, except the neckline, but their proportions were to be right for your figure.

More conventional clothing fits the body more exactly in several areas—the shoulder line should match the slant of your shoulder line; the armhole should match the circumference of your arm; the bust line should be the right width and come exactly at your bust line, and the shoulders of the garment should end just at your shoulder tips. Once you have a basic pattern that fits you properly in these strategic areas, you can use it as a basis for cutting out dozens of different garments. The *fit* of a garment depends on its dimensions; its *style* comes from the way in which the pattern is used. Once you know your own measurements exactly, and how they apply to a pattern, you will be able not only to cut your own patterns but to use commercial patterns more successfully.

Your body is, in essence, a column of a certain height and width. It is not a uniformly straight column, however, but one with various bulges and curves. It is surmounted by a head that rests on a neck that fits into shoulders, and the shoulders slant downward to join the arms. In order to make a good pattern for a blouse, dress, jacket, coat, robe, shirt, or any other garment that hangs from the shoulders, you must know the width of your shoulders and the slant of your shoulder line. You also need to know the location and measurements of your bust, waist, and hip line. For your convenience, take a sheet of paper and sketch a figure on it as shown in the drawing. When you have noted down on it the required measurements, you will have the basis for a **Chart of Measurements** from which many different patterns can be made. We will start with a simple sleeveless blouse, which will give you the beginning of all the other patterns.

BASIC BLOUSE

In Chapter 1, you measured the width across your shoulders and the distance from mid-shoulder to your waistline. Transfer those figures now to your chart. (If you've misplaced the measurements, turn to pages 4 and 5 and take them again.)

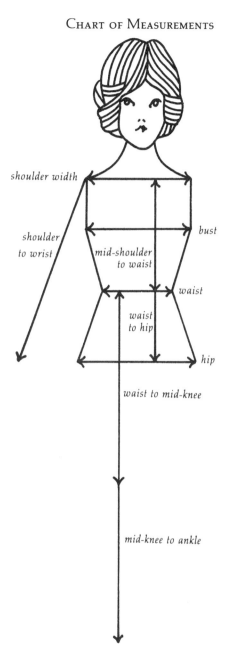

shoulder width

shoulder to wrist

mid-shoulder to waist

bust

waist

waist to hip

waist

hip

waist to mid-knee

mid-knee to ankle

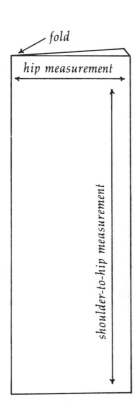

fold

hip measurement

shoulder-to-hip measurement

You now need to take your waist and hip measurements. Tie a string around your body at each of these places to get their exact location, remembering that your waist measurement is the smallest circumference in your body column and your hip measurement the largest below the waist. With the strings in place, measure around both areas and jot down the numbers on your chart. Measure from your waistline down the front of your body to your hip line and write down this measurement.

It is a little more difficult to measure the bust line, because it is hard to keep the string on a level line around your body. Put the string in place and then check its position in a mirror, from the front, side, and back until you are sure it is straight, then measure it.

These measurements are necessary to cut the rough pattern, and you will obtain the others from fitting the pattern itself. Use a large piece of muslin or similar material to make the pattern, as suggested in Chapter 2.

Begin by dividing the measurement of your hip line by four and adding 1½ inches. Fold your pattern material in half lengthwise to make a double section of material that wide. Add the measurement from your shoulder to your waist to the measurement from your waist to your hip line, add 3 inches, and mark a line that distance down from the top of the pattern material. This line indicates the bottom of your pattern. The material is now marked off roughly to indicate the width and length of the rectangle from which you will cut your pattern.

To make the shoulder line on the pattern, divide by two your total shoulder width and add 1 inch. With the center fold facing left, mark a point on the top of the pattern that distance from the upper left-hand corner. Mark a second point 1 inch below the first and draw a slanted line from the center fold to the second point. This makes a shoulder line with an average slant, which you will adjust to fit your own figure.

The next step is to mark the neckline. If you already have a permanent pattern for the fitted neckline (see Chapter 2), match its shoulder line to the high point of the shoulder line of this pattern, moving the neckline pattern down ⅝ of an inch to allow for seams. Sketch the front neckline on this pattern and cut around it. If you did not make the pattern for this neckline, do so now, following the directions on pages 20 and 21. Then, as above, sketch around it and, beginning at the neckline, cut a slit 4 inches long down the center fold.

You now have the width of your blouse, the length, the neckline, and the shoulder line. You need an armhole.

The average armhole is 6½ inches long. Its shape is a shallow curve that is deepest about 2½ inches from the bottom. Using one of two methods, you can make a pattern for an armhole based on these figures, and if your measurements are not close to the average, you can adjust the armhole later to fit you better.

One way to make an average pattern is to reproduce the armhole shown in the drawing using graph paper made from newspaper. Each small square on the drawing represents one square inch, and if you have never reproduced a design or a picture by this method, you will be surprised to find how easy it is.

To graph patterns, take a piece of newspaper and with a ruler and a crayon or felt-tip pen, mark it

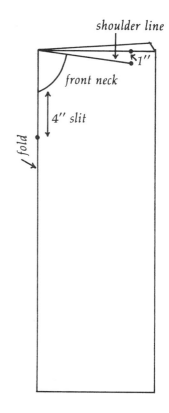

shoulder line

1″

front neck

4″ slit

fold

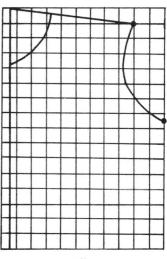

1 square = 1″

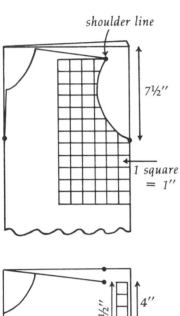

shoulder line

7½"

1 square = 1"

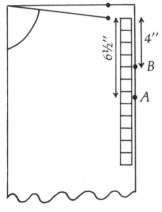

6½"

4"

B

A

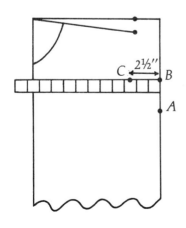

C   2½"   B

A

off in 1-inch squares. For the armhole pattern, a piece of newspaper a foot square will be large enough. Transfer the solid lines from the drawing to the newspaper. A good way to do this is to mark dots on the newspaper wherever the outline of the armhole crosses one of the lines on the graph. Then connect the dots, making sure that the relationship between your lines and your graph squares is the same as in the drawing. When you have finished, you will have an armhole pattern on the newspaper that is exactly the same proportions as the one in the drawing.

To transfer the armhole curve to the blouse pattern, mark a point on the side seam of the blouse pattern 7½ inches from the top of the cloth. Match up the base of the armhole pattern with this point and the top with the end of the shoulder line. Draw around the curve.

Another way to make an armhole pattern is to lay a ruler along the side edge of the blouse pattern with the top end of the ruler exactly even with the end of the shoulder line. Mark a point—A—on this side line 6½ inches below the end of the shoulder line.

Mark a second point—B—on this same line 4 inches below the end of the shoulder line. Turn your ruler so that it is at a right angle to the side line of the blouse and its edge is touching point B. Mark a third point—C—2½ inches to the left of the side line. Point C marks the deepest point in the curve of the armhole. With crayon or felt-tip pen, sketch a curve from the end of the shoulder line to point C, then from there to point A.

Cut out this pattern, which is for the blouse front, and fold another section of material to cut a back pattern the same size, but do not cut out the armhole and the neckline. Use your fitted neckline pattern to cut the back of the neckline, remembering to allow seam allowance at the shoulder line. For the armhole, make the curve shallower, with its deepest point 2 instead of 2½ inches from the bottom.

Baste the back and front of the pattern together at the shoulder seams with ⅝-inch seams. Slip the pattern over your head inside out. Pin the side seams with ⅝-inch seams, starting just under the armhole and aiming the points of the pins downward. You are now ready to adjust the pattern to fit you perfectly. Learning to do this will also help you to tell whether or not a ready-made blouse fits you, and if not, why not.

Look at yourself carefully in the mirror, beginning at the neckline. Does the pattern lie flat around your neck, or does it bulge? As before, you can fit this pattern more precisely if you do not leave seam allowance at the neckline. If there are bulges, remove them by pinning the shoulder seams deeper at the neckline. If this does not do the trick, pin a small tuck in the center back of the neckline and observe the results. Try lapping the center opening over if the front neckline is too loose. Mark any changes you make with chalk. If the neckline is too small, twist your neck around to make wrinkles in the excess material. These wrinkles can be marked with chalk to indicate where the neckline should be trimmed.

Check the fit of the shoulder seams. Do they follow your shoulder line closely, or do the ends of the seams stand up over your arm? Use pins to adjust the fit. If the shoulder seams bind, you can change the seams to give you more room—take out the stitches and pin new seams. Check especially to see that each

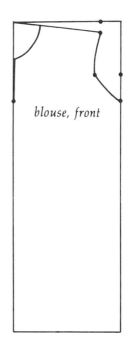

blouse, front

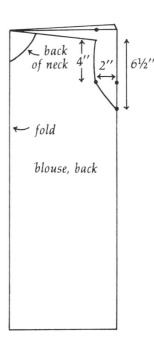

back of neck   4″   2″   6½″

fold

blouse, back

shoulder line (not including seam allowance, of course) ends exactly at the tip of your shoulder. A fitted shoulder line that droops over the arm is most unbecoming. Check each shoulder line separately, as your shoulders may not be identical.

What about the armholes? If they are too tight, see whether they should be cut deeper. Move your arms around to be sure that the armholes do not bind. If the armholes gap, it is because they are too big. This may mean that the curve is too deep, or that the armhole itself is too long. Check the blouse back as well as the front. Where does the armhole itself lie on your body? A good armhole reaches just to the top of the shoulder and curves under the arm at the bottom. Mark any necessary changes with chalk or pins.

Now for the side seams. You will probably find that the back needs to be narrower than the front, but be sure that the side seams run straight down your side if you make this change. The blouse itself should fit smoothly, without either bulging or pulling. The fit at the bust and hips affects this. Make changes in both areas to correct these problems if need be, experimenting until you have the fit right. If the blouse is too tight around the hips, it will "cup in" under the hip line. If it is too loose at the bust line, it will look bulky. Adjust the seams and check each adjustment in the mirror until you have a smooth, easy fit.

Stand well back from the mirror to get a good look at your whole figure to determine what blouse length is best for you. If your hips are wide, you will not want a blouse that emphasizes that part of your figure by ending exactly there. If you are short, you will find that a longer blouse gives you more apparent height. Try different lengths to find which one is most flattering to your figure. When the fitting has been completed, remove the pattern and make any necessary changes.

Your pattern is now complete. Trim the side and shoulder seams, leaving allowances for ⅝-inch seams. Mark the pattern "Basic Blouse" and note on it that there is no seam allowance at the armhole or neckline and no hem allowance. Since this is a basic pattern from which you will make different sorts of garments, tape the front slit together. For future use of the pattern, it will be helpful if you now draw a line across it marking your natural waistline, and another marking your hip line.

With your pattern pieces ready to use, you can go out and buy the material. It is easy to see that you will need enough material to cut two widths of the blouse whatever length you wish to make it. If the total width of both back and front is 45 inches or less, you need a piece of material the length of the blouse. If the total width is more than 45 inches, you need a piece of material twice the length of the blouse. If the blouse is to be an overblouse, add 2½ inches to the length for a hem; if it is to be a tucked-in model, add 6 inches. You also need enough additional yardage to make a bias binding for the neckline and both armholes, and a straight strip 11 inches long and 1½ inches wide for a continuous lap placket to finish the slit opening at the neck. The binding and the strip can be made from the same material as the blouse itself or from material in a contrasting color or pattern. If you need to buy two blouse lengths of the material for the blouse, you will have enough extra for the trimming. If you need to buy only one length,

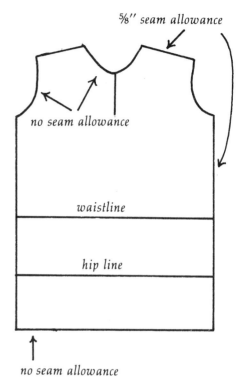

⅝" seam allowance

no seam allowance

waistline

hip line

no seam allowance

BASIC BLOUSE, FRONT

47

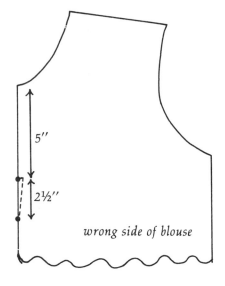

5″

2½″

wrong side of blouse

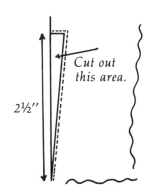

Cut out
this area.

2½″

you can use one of the ways of estimating material described in Chapter 2 to see if there will be enough left over for the trim. You will also need a spool of matching thread and a hook and eye for the neckline opening.

Before cutting the pattern from the material, check to see if the fabric is straight, as described in Chapter 1. If you have chosen a patterned material that has a design with an up and down to it, be sure to have the design running the same way on both the back and the front of the blouse.

Cut out the blouse, adding ¼-inch seam allowance at the neckline and armhole and whatever hem allowance you decided upon. Before sewing the blouse together, prepare to finish the neckline with a **continuous lap placket.** This is one of the handiest tricks you will learn in sewing, since it makes a neat, convenient, and tailored finish for a slit opening, and is very easy to do.

Fold the front of the blouse in half lengthwise, inside out, and cut a slit 5 inches deep down the center fold. With the front of the blouse still folded, mark a point 2½ inches below the slit. With the blouse still folded, stitch a horizontal line ¼ inch long under the very bottom of the slit. Turn the blouse in the machine and make a line of stitches from the end of the stitched line down to the point you marked. You are making a short seam in the front of the blouse, a trick that will make the continuous lap placket a cinch to apply. Take the blouse from the machine and cut a triangular piece out of the stitched area, beginning just below the horizontal row of stitches. The triangle should be cut right up to the end of the row of stitches, without cutting through it.

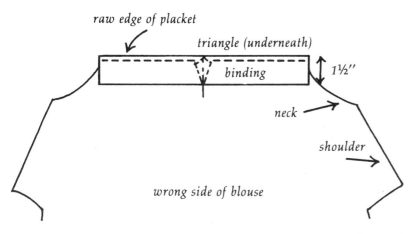

raw edge of placket

triangle (underneath)

binding

1½″

neck

shoulder

wrong side of blouse

On the straight of the material, cut the 1½- by 11-inch strip for the placket. The strip is to be sewn first to the wrong side, then folded over and stitched down to the right side of the blouse. Because of the triangle you cut out, you can open the slit to make a straight line for sewing. Lay the right side of the binding against the wrong side of the slit, match the raw edges, and sew in place with a ¼-inch seam. Turn the blouse over, fold the binding in half, and turn the raw edge under so that the strip just covers the first row of stitches. Stitch down. Fold the finished binding to the inside of the blouse; it will extend beyond the edge of the slit on one side, and fold back against the blouse on the other side to make a neat opening finish.

Now sew the shoulder seams and finish the neckline. To do the latter, cut a 1-inch wide strip of bias binding that is ½ inch longer than the length of the neckline including the placket extension on one side (see Chapter 2 for directions for making bias tape). Use it to make a **bias-binding inside facing** for the neckline.

To apply the facing, iron down a ¼-inch hem along one long edge of the bias binding. With right

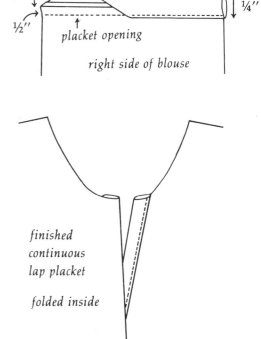

1¼″

¼″

½″

placket opening

right side of blouse

finished continuous lap placket

folded inside

sides together, sew the unironed edge of the binding to the neckline with a ¼-inch seam. The facing should extend ¼ inch beyond the neckline slit on each side. Turn back a ¼-inch hem at each end of the binding so that the facing is flush with the slit, and sew. Now with invisible stitches (see page 14), sew the long "hemmed" edge of the bias binding to the blouse.

Sew the side seams and then finish the armholes in the same way you did the neckline. Sew the hook and eye at the top of the neckline opening, turn up and sew a standard hem as described in Chapter 1, and your blouse is ready to wear.

A TENNIS SHIRT

You can use this same Basic Blouse pattern, with a shirt collar added, to make an attractive tennis shirt. (If you like, you can embroider or appliqué a golf club on it and call it a golfing shirt.) You also use the continuous lap placket somewhat differently. It is folded on the outside of the opening, so that it is on the right side of the blouse, and fastens with buttons and buttonholes.

The **shirt collar** requires a doubled piece of material 7 inches wide and 5 inches longer than the neckline. You can cut a permanent pattern for the collar from newspaper, since its fit depends upon its measurements and not upon how it fits your figure. Measure around the inside of the pattern neckline, add 5 inches, and cut a piece of paper that long and 7 inches wide. Fold the paper in half lengthwise, as the collar itself will be folded. The folded edge is the outside of the collar, and the open edge will be sewn

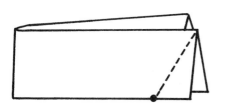

to the neckline. Fold the pattern in half crosswise. Mark a point 2 inches from the end on the open edge.

You are now ready to shape the front of the collar. The distinguishing characteristic of a standard shirt collar is that its corners are pointed. To make simple points, cut along a slanted line running from the mark you just made on the pattern to the outside folded end of the paper. Or if you like, you can round the corners of the collar, as the drawing indicates. You also may want to make the collar either wider or narrower than the suggested size—experiment with your paper pattern, look at yourself in the mirror, and decide what shape and size collar suits you best. The important thing is for the inside edge of the collar to fit the inside edge of the neckline perfectly. When you are satisfied with your pattern, cut it in half along the lengthwise fold. Label it "Shirt Collar" and be sure to mark on it "cut 2" and "no seam allowance." Then figure out how much material you will need for it and add that amount to your estimate.

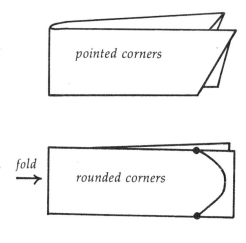

In estimating, remember to add hem allowance to the bottom of the shirt. You will also need enough scraps to cut a bias-binding facing for the neckline and armholes, and a straight strip for the placket opening. And you will need a spool of matching thread and two buttons. (If your fancy is caught by some odd-shaped or very large or very small buttons that are unsuited to buttonholes, you can use them as trim and buy snap fasteners to do the actual work.)

cut 2   no seam allowance

SHIRT COLLAR WITH POINTED CORNERS

cut 2   no seam allowance

SHIRT COLLAR WITH ROUNDED CORNERS

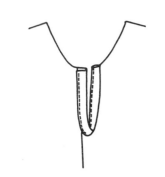

*finished continuous lap placket
folded outside*

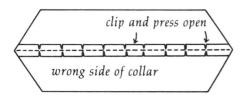

clip and press open

wrong side of collar

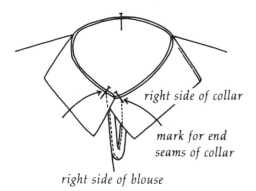

right side of collar

*mark for end
seams of collar*

right side of blouse

Cut the pattern pieces from the material, including a pocket if you want one. (See Chapter 2 for directions for making patch pockets.) Remember to add ½-inch seam allowance at the neckline and armholes and hem allowance at the bottom of the shirt. Add ½-inch seam allowance to all edges of the collar, and be sure that the collar is cut exactly on the straight of the cloth.

Make the shirt just as you did the basic blouse. Sew the continuous lap placket in the same way, but remember to fold it to the outside of the shirt. It should lap over the left side of the shirt. (Men's shirts lap over from left to right, women's from right to left.) You are now ready to **sew on your shirt collar.**

Pin the two sections of the collar together along the outside edge, right side of material to right side of material, and sew, using a ½-inch seam. Clip the seam (see Chapter 1), press it open, turn the collar right side out, and press again.

Measure the inside edge of the collar against the neckline of the shirt (pinning the middle of the collar to the middle of the back neckline and pinning in place from there to the neckline on each side). Place a pin in the neckline of the collar just where it reaches the seam of the front placket on each side. This is exactly where you want the end seams of the collar to be.

Remove the collar and stitch the end seams on the wrong side. Clip the corners, turn the collar right side out, and use a pin to pull the points out straight.

Cut a piece of bias binding long enough to go around the neckline with an inch to spare and prepare to make a "sandwich" of neckline, collar, and bias binding. Fit the collar on the right side of the neckline so that each end comes exactly to the seam of the placket opening. It will go over the placket extension on the left-hand side. If the collar does not fit exactly, its neckline can be made either larger or smaller. To make it larger, cut a curved section from the inside edge, as shown. To make it smaller, turn it wrong side out and restitch the end seams to take up the excess.

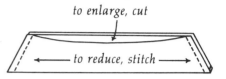

to enlarge, cut

to reduce, stitch

Place the bias-binding facing over the collar, right side of facing to right side of collar, and leave ½ inch of facing extending at each end. Pin the three layers securely in place, and stitch, using a ½-inch seam. Clip into the seam allowance as in Chapter 1 and trim away any excess material so that the seam won't look bunchy when you turn it. Turn the facing to the inside, tuck the ends under, and sew the facing to the shirt with invisible stitches.

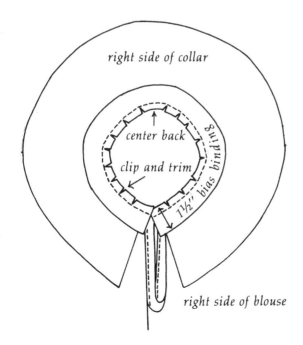

right side of collar

center back

clip and trim

1½" bias binding

right side of blouse

Continue making the shirt as before, sewing the side seams, finishing the armholes with a bias-binding inside facing, and finally hemming the shirt with a standard hem. Now you are ready for the fastenings.

If you are using buttons and buttonholes, **sew the buttons** to the bottom section of the placket. If you have fancy buttons, use snap fasteners for inside the placket and sew the buttons to the top section. Buttons are sewn to garments by hand, the fastening stitches forming what is called a shank. If you sew buttons too tightly to a garment, they are hard to button, so it is a good idea to make a shank as you sew. The length of the shank will depend on the thickness of the cloth; on this shirt, the shank does not need to be very long.

Line up the buttonholes over the underlap on the left front and make a chalk mark in the center of each buttonhole area to indicate exactly where the button should go. Take one or two loose stitches through the holes in the button to keep it in place, then lay a needle or pin under two sides of the button to hold it away from the cloth. Continue sewing on the buttons; the needles—or pins—will regulate the length of your stitches to make a short shank. (When sewing buttons on heavier materials, matches can be used, instead of needles or pins, to make a longer shank.)

To cut the buttonholes, measure the width of the button you plan to use, being sure you include the dimensions of the edges of the button in your measurement, and cut two slits in the top section of the placket just that long and exactly over the buttons. The slits should run up and down the placket, in the center of the width.

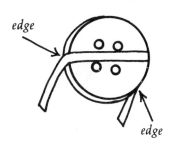

edge

edge

If your sewing machine has a buttonhole attachment, use it to stitch around the buttonholes, following the directions for your model. If not, you can **finish the buttonholes by hand,** which is rather tedious but makes them look great.

Thread a needle with double thread, wax the thread as in Chapter 1, and stitch all around the slit twice, about ⅛ inch from the edge, making very small stitches. This will stabilize the raw edge and give the buttonhole a good foundation.

The buttonhole stitch is a standard one, and easy to learn. Hide the knot by starting inside the layers of cloth around the buttonhole. Put the needle between the layers and bring it partway through ⅛ inch from the edge of the slit. Throw the thread to the left in a large loop and bring the needle and thread through, inside the loop. As you pull the thread through, a loop will automatically be formed over the edge of the buttonhole. Working from top to bottom, continue taking these stitches through both layers of material all the way around the buttonhole. The stitches should be very close together. Fan them out slightly at each end of the buttonhole.

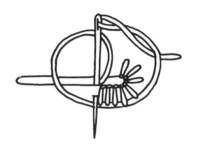

You now have made a Basic Blouse pattern and a variation of it. You have learned where and how a pattern fits, and how to cut out and sew together a shirt collar. You have learned to make a continuous lap placket and handmade buttonholes.

In the next chapter, you will use the Basic Blouse pattern to cut a full-length dress pattern.

· 4 ·

From Blouse to Dress:
An A-line Dress
and a Beach Cover-up

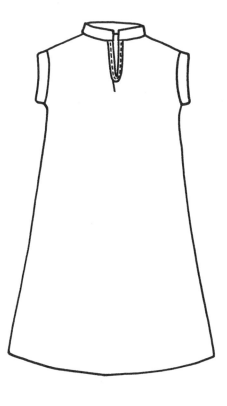

A-LINE DRESS

Sometimes the difference between a blouse and a dress is only a question of length. You can prove this by using your Basic Blouse pattern (see Chapter 3) to cut a basic A-line Dress pattern.

Fasten sheets of newspaper together to make a piece long enough for a dress pattern. With styles in the length of dresses changing as rapidly as they do, you must decide for yourself how long it should be. Mid-knee is a convenient length, since it is easy to make the pattern either longer or shorter for a specific garment.

Fold the front of the Basic Blouse pattern in half lengthwise, and position it on the newspaper so that the fold of the pattern is on the left-hand side of the paper. Mark around the blouse pattern with chalk or crayon. Now refer to your Chart of Measurements (see Chapter 3) and find your hip measurement and the distance from your shoulder to your hip line. Draw a line across the pattern at your hip line. (If this line is already marked on your Basic Blouse pattern, simply transfer it to the new pattern.) Divide your hip measurement by 4, add 2 inches, and mark a point on the hip line this distance from the left-hand edge of the paper.

Now stand in front of a mirror with a tape measure, hold one end of the tape measure at midpoint on one of your shoulders, and let the rest of it hang free. Notice the numeral on the tape measure that coincides with where you want the finished hemline to be. Draw a line across the pattern at this same distance down from the mid-shoulder point on the pattern.

Next you must make a new side seam for the A-line dress. With a yardstick draw a line from a point just at the bottom of the armhole through the point you marked on the hip line to the hemline of the dress. Cut out the pattern.

Repeat the process with the back of the blouse pattern, and you have the complete pattern for an A-line dress. In this case you will not need to make a cloth pattern—the A-line dress presents no new fitting problems; the parts that need to be fitted you fitted when you made the blouse pattern. Label both pieces of this pattern correctly for your permanent collection. Remember to mark them "no seam allowance" at the neckline and armhole and "no hem allowance" at the bottom of the pattern.

If your dress is going to be less than 45 inches long, you can make an A-line that is cut crosswise of the material (see Chapter 1) and thus save a great deal of

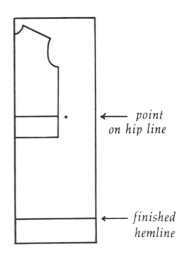

point on hip line

finished hemline

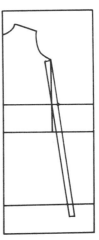

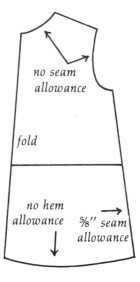

no seam allowance

fold

no hem allowance

⅝" seam allowance

fabric. Simply measure the width of the dress, front and back, at the hemline, translate this figure into yards, and buy that amount of material.

A number of different collars look good on this style of dress. Either the stand-up collar from Chapter 2 or the shirt collar from Chapter 3 would be fine. If you use the stand-up collar, you can put a matching stand-up binding around the armholes. The collar will require a strip of material 4 inches in width and the length of the neckline plus 1 inch. Each sleeve will require a strip 4 inches wide and the length of the entire armhole plus 1 inch. A binding this wide, when used to finish an armhole, makes a sleevelike finish. If you use the shirt collar, you can finish the armholes with a bias-binding inside facing, as you did the basic blouse.

Estimate the amount of material you will need for the collar and facing and for the binding at the armholes, and see if you will have any scraps of leftover dress material you can use. If not, estimate how much more fabric you must buy. You will also need a package of seam binding, a spool of matching thread, and a snap fastener.

The dress itself is so easy to make it might be called a zip dress. Cut out the material, adding a ½-inch seam allowance at the neckline and armhole and a 3-inch hem allowance. Fold the front of the dress in half lengthwise and cut a slit 5 inches deep down the center fold. Finish the opening with a continuous lap placket (see Chapter 3).

Sew the shoulder seams, then sew on either the stand-up collar (see Chapter 2) or the shirt collar (see Chapter 3).

Try the dress on and look at yourself in the mirror

to see if you want to change the side seams before sewing them. You can make the dress narrower, if that is more becoming to you, but don't make it so narrow that it is no longer an A-line.

Sew the side seams, then finish the armholes. If you are using a bias-binding inside facing, follow the directions in Chapter 3 for applying it. If you are using a **stand-up binding** at the armholes, turn the dress wrong side out and beginning at the underarm seam, lay one of your strips of binding on an armhole with the edges matching, right side of binding to wrong side of dress. Pin in place, and when you have pinned the binding completely around the armhole, mark the points on each end of the binding where they meet at the side seam. Unpin enough of the binding to sew a seam at these points across the ends of the binding. Now sew the binding in place around the armhole.

Turn the dress right side out and fold the binding in half. Turn the raw edge of the binding under and stitch down just over the first row of stitches. Do the same to the other armhole.

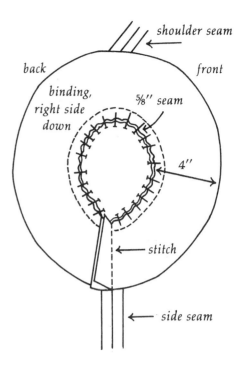

shoulder seam

back   front

binding, right side down

⅝" seam

4"

stitch

side seam

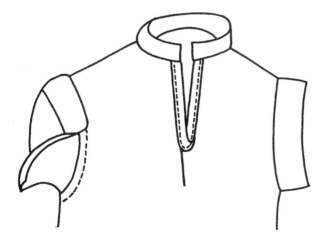

You are now ready to hem your dress. Put the dress on, stand in front of a mirror, and mark where you want the finished hemline to be. Take the dress off, put it on a hanger, and suspend it in an open doorway. Pin the hem in place all the way around the dress, then press it.

Note that the turned-up edge of the hem is wider around than the part of the dress to which the edge is to be sewn. You take care of this by making a row of **gathering stitches** around the hem edge to make it the proper size. The gathering stitches can be made either by machine or by hand. In using the machine, set it for the longest possible stitch, and when working by hand, use a double thread and take stitches 1 inch in length.

In any case, make a separate row of gathering stitches on the back and the front of the hem edge, leaving extra thread at both ends of each row. Now turn the dress wrong side out, lay it out flat, pin up the hem, and pull up the thread on each row of stitches until the hem fits the body of the dress perfectly, spreading the gathers evenly along the entire row.

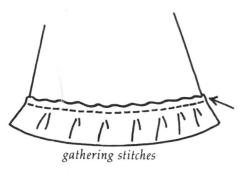

gathering stitches

On this dress you will use a **standard hem with seam binding.** Seam binding is used on a hem any-time the fabric is too heavy for a raw edge to be turned under, or when the hem is too bulky, as it is when it has been gathered. Unpin the hem and sew the seam binding in place over the gathering stitches, so that the binding covers the raw edge. Remove the gathering stitches. Pin the hem in place, then sew it with invisible stitches (see Chapter 1).

Put the snap fastener in at the neckline, and your A-line dress is ready to wear. You will find it a useful addition to your wardrobe, so useful that you will probably want to make several for summer wear.

BEACH COVER-UP

The same A-line Dress pattern is also excellent for a beach cover-up made of terry cloth. You may want to make the cover-up shorter than the dress, use an oval neckline as you did on the peasant blouse in Chapter 1, and finish the neckline, armholes, and bottom with bias binding (see Chapter 2). Buy enough colorful terry cloth for the cover-up, then see if you have enough permanent-press material left from one of your other projects to make the bias binding. You don't need directions for sewing the garment because you've already learned every step required.

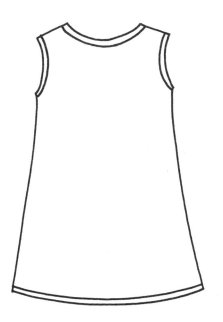

· 5 ·

Becoming Serious About Fit: A Tailored Shirt with Darts

Because the clothes in the first four chapters were lightly fitted, no darts were required, but you need to know how to make darts if you are to become a really accomplished seamstress. There are usually side-seam darts in ready-made clothing and in garments made from commercial patterns, and it may seem to you that there is no basic theory behind their size and position, that they are just set in at random. This, however, is not really true.

If you take an orange in your hand and try to wrap a paper napkin around it, you will discover that the only way the napkin can cover the curved fruit is to fold into wrinkles. The human body has a number of curves and bulges around which cloth will not fit without folding into wrinkles. Darts are really nothing more than properly placed and stitched-down wrinkles that make a garment fit.

The purpose of darts in the side seams of blouses and dresses is to make the garment fit over the curve of the bust line without bulging out over the flatter areas of the torso. The most common darts are short ones, set in the side seams just opposite the bust line. These darts are to take up extra material that would otherwise bulge or wrinkle; they should point directly at the highest point of the bust, and they should fold down flat along their entire length. Unless such darts conform to these standards, they are a failure. You can see how many poor darts there are in the world by checking those in your present clothing and in clothing worn by others. Since no two figures are exactly the same, it is impossible for darts in mass-produced clothing to fit properly.

Not all blouses, shirts, and dresses require darts, but there will always be some garments in which you will want them. Here is the way to **design side-seam darts** to fit your own figure.

Get out your pattern for the front of the basic blouse (Chapter 3), fold it lengthwise, and place it on a piece of muslin or other pattern-cutting material that you have folded lengthwise, so you can cut out a complete front. Draw around the neckline, shoulder line, armhole, and side seam. Make this pattern 3 inches longer than the one for the basic blouse.

With a yardstick or ruler, mark a point—A—on the side seam 3 inches down from the bottom of the armhole and another point—B—1½ inches to the right of the first one. Use a yardstick or ruler to draw a line from the bottom of the armhole to point B. Draw another line from point B to a third point—C—about 6 inches below the bottom of the armhole. Cut out the pattern, including the triangular section you just

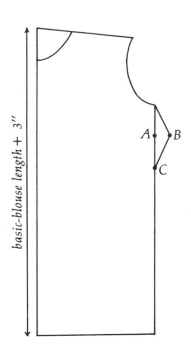

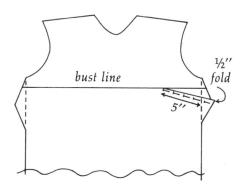

bust line

½″ fold

5″

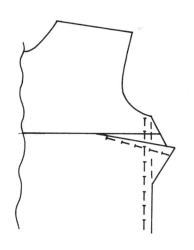

drew on the side seam. Then measure from the middle of your shoulder line down to the highest point of your bust; open out the pattern, and draw a line across the pattern this distance from the shoulder line.

Now cut a pattern for the back, using your pattern for the back of the basic blouse. The only change will be the addition of 3 inches at the bottom. Baste the patterns for the blouse front and the blouse back together at the shoulder seams, and slip on the basted pattern, inside out. Fold the extra material on each side of the front of the pattern into a side-seam dart. To do this, first fold in half the extra pointed sections. Begin with a dart about ½ inch wide at the top or, in other words, one that takes up about 1 inch of fabric. Each dart should be about 5 inches long and should taper to a point. Angle the dart upward so that it points at the highest point of your bust. Pin the darts in place and pin the side seams together below the darts. Check the results from the front and from each side. What you want to create with the darts is a garment that follows the curves of your body more closely than the basic blouse does; what you don't want is too tight a fit. If too much material has been taken in, meaning the darts are too large or too long, repin them. If the darts are too small, repin them to use all the excess material. Always check the entire appearance of the pattern after each change, to be sure that altering the size or shape of the darts has not spoiled the rest of the pattern's fit. When you think the darts are right, pin the tops of the side seams together to see how the garment will look when they are sewn. Adjust the darts again if necessary. The front pattern will now be shorter than the

64

back, so mark the bottom where you will cut to even it up.

Unpin one side seam and take off the pattern. Be sure that the dart seam is pinned along its entire length. With the dart still pinned, trim the side seam to a straight line, removing the excess material at the dart area. Now unpin the dart, and draw along the lines where the pins were and down the fold line to make a record of the position of the dart. Do the same to the other dart. This is the pattern for the front of the fitted blouse, to be used with the pattern you cut for the back. Label the pattern "Fitted Blouse with Darts" and mark it carefully for your permanent collection, including "no seam allowance" at the neck and armholes, "⅝-inch seam allowance" at the shoulder and side seams, and "no hem allowance." For future use, draw a line across the pattern indicating where your natural waistline is.

This pattern can be used with any kind of material, but it is most useful with fabric that is not too soft or flexible. Soft, flexible materials that drape easily do not really require darts for fitting. The pattern can be easily adapted to make a tailored shirt, which is a useful addition to any wardrobe.

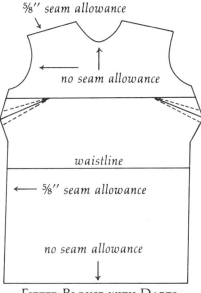

Fitted Blouse with Darts

TAILORED SHIRT

This tailored shirt buttons down the front and has a shirt collar and a shirt pocket with flap. The front opening will require extra material, as will the collar and pocket, so in order to know how much fabric to buy, you will need to check the measurements for the front and have patterns for the collar and pocket.

You probably already have a pattern for the collar,

65

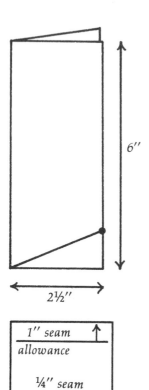

Shirt Pocket

since it is the same as the Shirt Collar pattern for the tennis shirt in Chapter 3. If you did not make a pattern then, do so now. The pattern for the **shirt pocket with flap** can also be cut from newspaper, since it, like the pattern for the collar, is flat and does not need to be fitted to you.

Begin with two pieces of newspaper, each 5 inches wide and 6 inches long. Fold one piece, which will be the pocket, in half lengthwise. With the fold facing left, mark a point on the right-hand edge 1 inch from the bottom. Draw a slanted line from that point to the bottom of the folded edge. Cut along the line, and you have a shirt pocket pattern with a pointed bottom. Label the pattern "Shirt Pocket" and mark it "1-inch seam allowance" at the top and "¼-inch seam allowance" on all other edges.

To make the pattern for the flap of the pocket, fold the other piece of paper in half crosswise, then fold the paper in half lengthwise, and with the folds at the top and facing left, mark a point on the right-hand edge 1 inch from the bottom. Draw a line from there to the bottom of the folded edge. When you cut along the line, you will have a flap of double thickness with the same pointed bottom as the pocket. Label the pattern "Shirt Pocket, flap," mark the crosswise fold line, and mark the pattern "¼-inch seam allowance" on all edges.

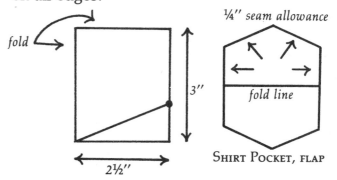

Shirt Pocket, flap

The shirt front is to be cut 5 inches wider than the Fitted Blouse pattern, to provide material for finishing the front opening. With this information, you are ready to estimate how much yardage you will need. The shirt can be made out of any wash-and-wear fabric, and the pattern can be cut either lengthwise or crosswise on the material. You will also need buttons for the front opening, spaced 3 inches apart along the length of the shirt front. Fold the pattern in half and starting ½ inch below the neckline, mark a dot every three inches, then count the dots to see how many buttons you will need. A regular shirt button is plain and white with a ½ inch diameter, but you can choose whatever kind you like. The only requirement is that they be easy to button—not the ornamental type that looks pretty but is hard to fasten. You will also need a spool of matching thread.

To cut the shirt from the material, fold the fabric so that it is 2½ inches wider than the folded pattern for the shirt front. Lay the shirt front pattern on the material, 2½ inches back from the folded edge. Draw a straight horizontal line to extend the bottom of the neckline to the edge of the material. Remember to add seam allowance to the neckline and armholes and ½-inch allowance for a narrow hem at the bottom.

When the front has been cut, and while it is still folded, mark a point on the side seam 3 inches up from the bottom and another on the bottom edge 3 inches away from the side seam. Draw a curved line that connects these two points. Cut along the line to round the bottom edge of the shirt.

Cut the shirt front in half down the center fold. On the right-hand front, draw a vertical line 2 inches away from the center line, and cut away this strip.

67

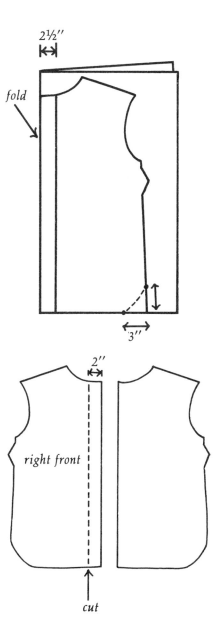

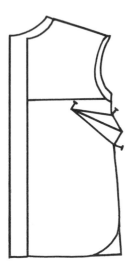

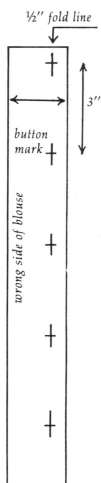

½″ *fold line*

3″

button mark

wrong side of blouse

Now you will need to transfer your dart markings from the pattern to the shirt. Place the pattern on one side of the shirt with the side seams lined up, but with the pattern below the ½-inch seam allowance you have added to the shirt. Put a pin through each side of the top of the dart and one through the bottom of the dart. Turn the pattern and shirt over carefully, so that the pins are not dislodged, and mark these three points on the shirt with chalk. These marks should be sufficient guides to sew the darts, but if you wish you can use them only as guidelines to draw in the complete sewing lines. Repeat with the dart on the other half of the shirt front.

Cut out the back of the shirt and round the bottom corners the same way you did on the front.

On this shirt, you will use **easy bound buttonholes,** which are much less tedious to make than regular bound buttonholes. They are formed in a seam and require no cutting.

To make the buttonholes, begin by pressing a ½-inch hem down one long edge of the strip of material you cut from the right-hand side of the shirt. Unfold the hem and use chalk to reproduce the buttonhole marks you made on the shirt front on this edge of the material. The marks should be on the wrong side and exactly on the fold line. Measure across one of your buttons to learn its diameter—be sure to include the dimensions of the edges of the button in your measurement—and chalk a vertical line this long through every button mark, using the original mark as the center of the line. The vertical lines represent the buttonholes and are your guides for the next step.

Fold the strip in half lengthwise, creasing the fold,

then place the opened out strip on the right-hand side of the shirt front, right side of strip to right side of shirt. Position the strip as shown, so that the edge near which you made the guidelines for the buttonholes is even with the center edge of the shirt. You are going to stitch the strip to the shirt along the first fold line on the strip, making a ½-inch seam, leaving the marked buttonhole lines unsewn. Stitch up and down a few times at the beginning and end of each open buttonhole to make the seam more secure.

Press the seam open, then fold the strip in half along the second fold line and turn under the raw edge ½ inch so that the fold just meets the seam line. Stitch along the edge of this fold, skipping the buttonholes on the way. Now, for further security, on the right side of the shirt, stitch around each buttonhole ⅛ inch from the edge, forming your stitches in an oblong.

One element of successful sewing is learning how to handle different kinds of material to achieve a well-made finished product. If you were making a coat of heavy, loosely woven material, for example, you might find it difficult to make good-looking buttonholes by finishing them as in Chapter 3, either by hand or on your machine with a buttonhole stitch. Regular bound buttonholes would be difficult to make because of the weight of the material. This is one of the situations in which easy bound buttonholes are useful, since they give a tailored appearance when finished and can be easily made in almost any material. Keep this in mind as you sew, and when you tackle any new problem stop and think what technique you can use to achieve the effect you

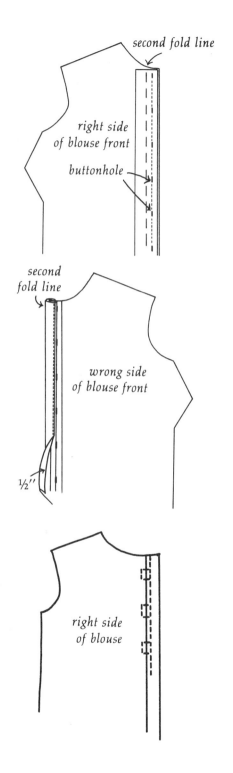

second fold line

right side
of blouse front

buttonhole

second
fold line

wrong side
of blouse front

½″

right side
of blouse

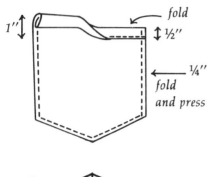

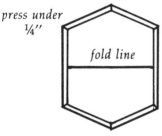

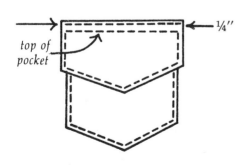

desire. No one technique is right for every garment you make, and the more alternatives you know the better your work will be.

After the buttonholes are finished, sew the shoulder seams and both darts. Put the shirt on, lap the right front over the extension on the left front, stand in front of a mirror, and decide where you want the pocket to be. Mark the place with chalk.

Putting the pocket and flap on the shirt at this stage is the next logical step. To make the pocket, fold under the top edge 1 inch and turn under the raw edge ½ inch. Stitch. Fold under the other outside edges of the pocket ¼ inch, and press in place. Pin the pocket to the shirt where you want it to be, and sew, beginning at the top of one side and ending at the top of the other side. Stitch back and forth several times at the beginning and the end of the seam for security. So far this is much like the patch pocket in Chapter 2.

Fold the pocket flap in half along the fold line, and press under the outside edges ¼ inch. Be sure that the finished width of the flap is the same as the width of the finished pocket. Stitch around the outside edges of the flap. Pin it in place just above the pocket, with the top edge of the flap ¼ inch above the top edge of the pocket. Stitch in place along the top edge.

Fold a hem down the center edge of the left front of the shirt, making two 1-inch folds. This makes a hem with three layers of material, which is a good sturdy foundation for buttons. Stitch this hem in place.

Fold the shirt collar in half lengthwise, right sides together, and measure it to be sure it fits the neckline of the blouse. It should extend to the center front on each side, which will be the buttonhole seam on the

70

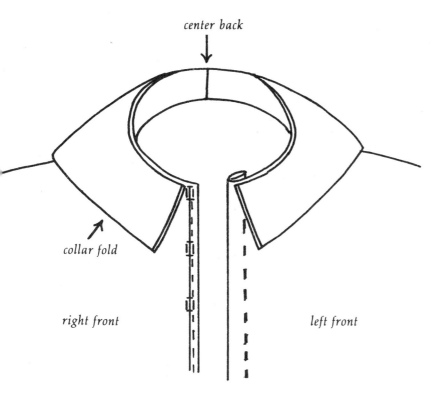

center back

collar fold

right front

left front

right side of the shirt and the middle of the hemmed edge of the left side. Mark a seam on each end of the collar that will make the collar exactly the same size as the neckline. Sew these seams and cut off the excess material at the point on each side. Turn the collar right side out, and stitch around the outside edge as shown.

The collar is put on the shirt sandwich fashion, as before (see Chapter 3). Cut a strip of bias binding 1 inch wide and 1 inch longer than the neckline of the shirt including the ½ inch that extends beyond the collar on both fronts. Mark the center of the bias tape with a pin. Fold the back of the shirt to locate the center of the back of the neckline, and mark this spot with a pin. Fold the collar in half, crosswise, and

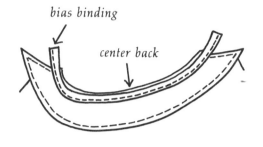

bias binding

center back

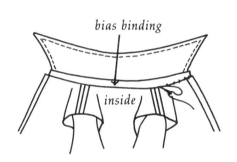

bias binding

inside

mark its center with a pin. Lay the collar on the neckline on the right side of the shirt, and the bias tape on top of the collar, using the pins to center them. The ends of the collar should reach exactly to the ends of the neckline and the bias tape should extend beyond the extensions.

Sometimes when you reach this point you are horrified to discover that in spite of all your careful measuring, the collar is either too large or too small. You know by now what to do—check back to page 51.

Sew the collar in place, stitching all the way to the ends of the bias binding. Clip all around the neckline. Fold the ends of the bias tape in; then turn the tape to the inside of the shirt. Trim off any excess material in the seam, and stitch the tape down with invisible stitches, being careful not to cover the top buttonhole.

Make a **shirttail hem** around the bottom of the shirt. This is simply a narrow hem folded over ¼ inch twice and stitched down by machine. Next finish the armholes with a bias-binding inside facing (see Chapter 3). Now sew up the side seams of the shirt, sew on the buttons, and your shirt is finished.

· 6 ·

Moving on to Skirts: A Sports Skirt and a Straight Skirt

The best way to begin thinking about skirt patterns is to look upon a skirt as a fitted tube. If the body were a straight column, one could cut out a piece of material the right dimensions, sew it into a tube, put it on, and that would be that. A properly made skirt, however, has to fit at both the waistline and at the hip line, which are different in size, and has to allow room for the legs in walking, which is where adjustment comes in. A good place to begin is with a **Basic A-line Skirt pattern.**

To make the pattern, you need a sheet of newspaper, a yardstick, a crayon, and three of the measurements from your Chart (see Chapter 3). The left-hand side of the newspaper will be the center front line of the pattern.

Divide your waist measurement by 4, add 3, and mark a point—A—on the top edge of the paper that

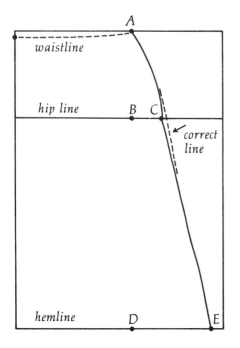

distance from the left-hand side. Mark a point—B— directly below this representing the distance from your waistline to your hip line. Draw a line across the paper at this point. Divide your hip measurement by 4, add 3, and mark a point—C—on the hip line this far from the left-hand side of the paper. Since a knee-length skirt is a good basic model—you can shorten or lengthen the pattern depending on current styles—measure from your waistline to a point just below your kneecap and on the paper mark a point—D—this distance from the waistline. (Remember to add the figure to your measurement chart.) Draw a line across the paper at that point to represent the hemline. Mark a point—E—on the hemline 4 inches to the right of point C on the hip line, as shown in the drawing.

Connect the points A and C with a curved line, then use the yardstick to continue this line to point E on the hemline. Correct the line so that the change from curved to slanted line is not too abrupt.

A slightly curved waistline fits better than a straight one, so mark a point on the left-hand side of the paper ½ inch down from the top and draw a new waistline that curves between this point and the side seam of the skirt as shown. Cut out the pattern.

You now need to cut both front and back of your basic skirt pattern from muslin or other pattern-cutting material, using the newspaper pattern for both. Cut each from folded material, with the center front and center back lines on the fold, and mark the center lines on each. Cut the skirt front in two down the center fold.

Pin the two front halves together, making a ⅝-inch seam.

The curved side line between waist and hip line helps shape the skirt, but vertical **darts at the waistline** are also needed to make it really fit. You should pin these darts before trying on the skirt pattern, since it is easier to make them the basic size and in the basic position while the material is still flat. Make a tapered, vertical dart ½ inch wide at the top and 3½ inches long, on each side of the front of the skirt 3 inches from the center.

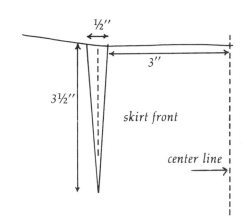

Make two more vertical darts, one on each side of the back of the skirt 3½ inches from the center, 6 inches long and ¾ inch wide at the top.

To fit the pattern properly, you will need a half slip. Fold the slip in half, matching the side seams, mark its exact center front and back with pins, and put on the slip. With the wrong side out, pin the center of each pattern piece to the exact center of the slip, front and back.

Start fitting the side seams for a smooth fit between waistline and hip, pinning both sides the same amount. Adjust each seam along its entire length for a smooth line. Since this is an A-line skirt, the side seams slant out from the hip line to the hem, but you do not want an exaggerated flare. After pinning, take a few steps to be sure the bottom of the skirt is wide enough for easy walking. Check frequently to be sure the side seams will make a straight line down the center of your sides.

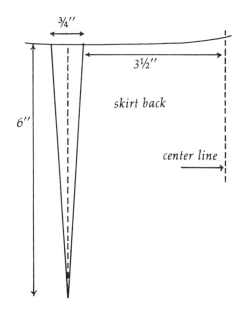

It is now time to check the darts. They may be the wrong size or in the wrong position. Their purpose is to make the skirt fit smoothly, and if it is either too tight or too loose, if it wrinkles or is too bulky, the fault lies in the darts. Change both sets of matching darts each time in the same way until you are

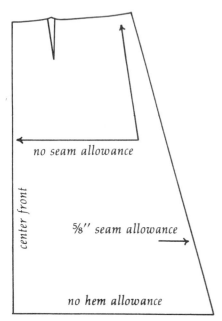

no seam allowance

center front

⅝" seam allowance

no hem allowance

BASIC A-LINE SKIRT, FRONT

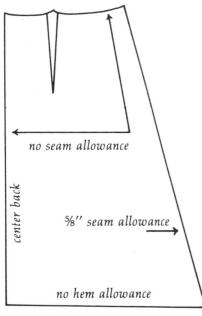

no seam allowance

center back

⅝" seam allowance

no hem allowance

BASIC A-LINE SKIRT, BACK

satisfied with the result. You are then ready to check the waistline. You will not leave a seam allowance at the waistline. Bend forward and backward and from side to side to see how these movements affect the pattern. Creases caused by bending will indicate that the curve of the waistline needs to be changed. Chalk the changes. You will probably find it helpful to leave a small triangle of material above each dart when you trim the waistline.

Unpin the pattern from the slip, unpin the front opening down 7 inches from the top, and take off the pattern. Mark any necessary changes in the side seams and then unpin them. Put the two front halves of the skirt together, making sure that they match exactly. Fold the back of the skirt in half lengthwise and check to see that the side seams match. When trimming the side seams, allow ⅝-inch seam allowance. Trim the waistline on the chalked line. Mark the darts, front and back, as on pages 67 and 68.

You are now ready to make a permanent Basic A-line Skirt pattern. You need to make only half the back and half the front, so cut the pattern for the back in half down the center. Select one half of the skirt front as a permanent pattern, and trim the ⅝-inch seam allowance from the center front. Mark "no seam allowance" along the center line and at the waistline of each pattern and "no hem allowance" at the bottom. Mark "⅝-inch seam allowance" at the side seam of each. Label the patterns "Basic A-line Skirt Back," and "Basic A-line Skirt Front."

SPORTS SKIRT

The first skirt to make with your A-line Skirt pattern

is a sports model with lined saddle pockets, a full-length front zipper, and an inside facing at the waistline. Using newspaper, make graph paper with 1 inch squares, and following the directions in Chapter 3 for graphing patterns, copy the pattern for the **saddle pocket.** Cut two pocket patterns from newspaper, so you can check to see if their size is right for you. This beginning pattern has no seam allowances.

The top seam of the saddle pockets will be sewn into the waistband of the skirt, and their short side seam will be sewn into the side seams of the skirt. Pin the pocket patterns in place on whatever garment you happen to be wearing to see whether you would like to make them either larger or smaller. Before making any changes, think about the use of the pockets, as well as their appearance. The curved line on the outside is the opening, which must be large enough for your hand to fit comfortably. The straight inside edge of the pocket is its length, and the portion at the bottom should be deep enough to hold whatever you want to put there. If you make the pocket shorter, remember to leave the opening and the actual body of the pocket large enough for use. If you make it narrower, trim from the straight inside edge, not from the outside edge, so that the opening doesn't become too large.

When your pocket patterns suit you, cut a duplicate of one of them for your permanent collection, adding ½ inch for seams to all edges. Label the pattern "Saddle Pocket" and mark it "½-inch seam allowance" on all edges. The pockets are lined, and the lining is cut from the same pattern as the pocket itself.

The skirt and pockets should be made of some

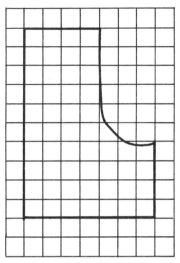

1 square = 1″

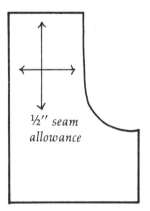

½″ seam
allowance

SADDLE POCKET

moderately heavy material, such as denim, duck, or similar sports fabric, and the pocket linings can be of any wash-and-wear material. You might want to make a navy-blue denim skirt with pocket linings of red-and-white striped material, and a full-length red zipper in the front. In that case the full-length zipper would be part of the decoration of the skirt, and should therefore be a fairly large one with an open end, the kind of zipper used for jackets and other garments that need to be opened completely to remove them. The price of a zipper is based upon its size and length, so you should take this into consideration before deciding which kind to buy.

Zippers are nothing more than convenient devices for closing openings in garments. Such openings are put into garments so the garments can be put on and taken off easily. Your skirt, for example, needs such an opening because it is smaller at the waist than at the hips and would not go on without one.

For most garments, it is wise to remember that using an unnecessary zipper, or one longer than necessary, is a needless expense. You can save a great deal of money by making garment openings no more than the required length and buying zippers that fit them exactly. This is easy to do with patterns that you design yourself, and you can also adjust commercial patterns to avoid spending more money than you have to.

Figure out what the zipper is for and what length it really needs to be. It is foolish, for instance, to spend money on a zipper that goes all the way down the back of a blouse when all that is really required is one long enough to allow the neckline to go over your head easily.

In most skirts the zipper is between 5 and 9 inches long, but in the case of this skirt, an unnecessarily long, full-length zipper with an open end is used for two reasons. It will enhance the appearance of the skirt, and can be put in as an "in-seam" zipper, which is the easiest type to sew into a garment. It is the best kind to use when you are learning to put in a zipper, and a great way to lose your fear of sewing one in if you have already had zipper problems.

Open-end zippers come in every imaginable length, so you need to know how long yours is to be before buying it. Lay your skirt front pattern on the floor, or on a table, and decide exactly how long you want the skirt to be. Then get out a tape measure. The top of the zipper is to come 1½ inches below the waistline, so begin measuring from there. The zipper itself will extend all the way to the hemline of your skirt, or it can end two or three inches above it. Basing the length of your zipper on these facts, take the measurement, jotting down the right size on a piece of paper.

In estimating how much material to buy for the skirt, keep in mind that you must have enough for the skirt's front and back, the two pockets, and the facing at the waistline, which should be a strip 2 inches wide and the length of the waistline plus 1 inch. (Cut the facing after the skirt is sewn so that you can match it properly to the waistline.) You will also need a small amount of another material for the pocket linings. To be sure your estimate is correct, you will probably need to draw fabric dimensions on the floor with chalk, as in Chapter 2. Three inches are to be added to the center front of each side of the skirt for a zipper facing and 3 inches to the length you

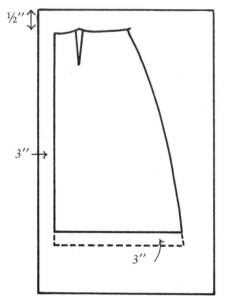

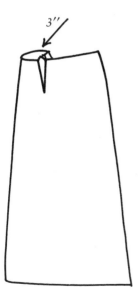

have chosen for the skirt. Since the skirt front is open down the center, you can cut out each half separately if it is more convenient or economical. You will also need the zipper, a spool of matching thread, a package of seam binding, and a hook and eye for the top of the skirt opening.

To cut out the skirt, place the Skirt Front pattern 3 inches away from the edge of your material and ½ inch down from the top. At the waistline cut the material ½ inch above the pattern waistline, follow the side seams exactly, and cut the bottom line of the skirt 3 inches below the length you want the skirt to be. If you cut both halves of the front of the skirt at the same time on folded material, cut the skirt front in half down the center fold. The back pattern is cut with the center back line on a fold. Don't forget to add seam allowance at the waistline and hem allowance at the bottom. Mark the darts, front and back, as on page 68.

The first principle for **putting in an in-seam zipper** is the same as that of finishing any opening in a garment—do it before the main seams of the garment have been sewn, so that you are working with a flat area and not inside a tube. That is why, in making this skirt, putting in the zipper is the first step after cutting.

Fold each skirt front under 3 inches, with the turn-under toward the wrong side of the material. Turn each raw edge under ¼ inch and stitch it.

Crease the folded edges with your fingers, pin in place, or press them with an iron. Open the zipper to separate the two parts and place one half of it under the corresponding edge of the fold in the skirt front. Place the top of the zipper 2 inches down from the top of the skirt and pin it in place. (If the zipper lock is on this side, push it down to the bottom of the zipper.) Fold the top end of the zipper tape under, and set the zipper in place, so that the folded edge of the material reaches almost to the teeth of the zipper. This will allow a small strip of the tape to show when the skirt is zipped, providing a decorative note. (It is possible, when inserting an in-seam zipper, to bring both folded edges of the cloth to the exact middle of the zipper teeth, thus hiding the zipper completely. The trouble with this method is that the material of the fold is always catching in the zipper teeth when you zip, which is a real nuisance.)

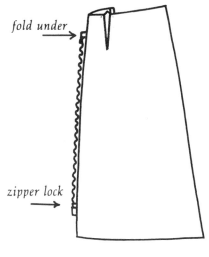

fold under →

zipper lock →

You will need to fasten the zipper in place along its entire length before you sew it, and there are several ways to do this. You can baste it, of course, or you can pin it—in the latter case, you will have to remove the pins directly ahead as you stitch. A third method is to buy special tape that is made to hold zippers in place. The instructions for using this tape come with the package. You need to be careful to place the tape so that you do not sew through it as you stitch the zipper, because the glue from the tape can gum up your needle. A final method is to use regular cellophane tape to hold the outside cloth edge of the zipper in place—again, to avoid gumming your needle be sure not to stitch over it. Whichever method you use, make certain the zipper lies perfectly flat and even.

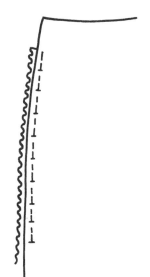

You can perfectly well use the regular presser foot on most sewing machines to sew in this or any other kind of zipper; you do not need to use a special zipper foot. On the right side of the skirt, start stitching from the top toward the bottom, and if this side of

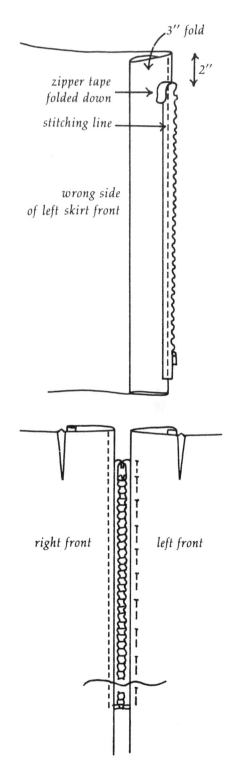

3" fold

2"

zipper tape
folded down

stitching line

wrong side
of left skirt front

right front

left front

the zipper has the lock on it, stop stitching before you reach it, at a point where the machine needle is *in* the material. Lift the presser foot, move the zipper lock up past the needle, lower the presser foot, and continue stitching to the end of the zipper.

By following these directions, you should be able to do a perfect job the first time, but if you don't, do not worry. Just take the zipper out and do it over. If you made mistakes, you can easily see what they are, and this is the best time to correct them. Another comfort is that once you have learned to sew in a zipper properly, you will retain the skill forever, and putting in zippers will never be a problem to you. The other ways of setting in a zipper, which are described later—lapped and in a fly front—are just as easy as this. The only difference is in the way the material itself is handled and not in the way the zipper is sewn.

The other side of the zipper is put in the same way, with the folded edge of the skirt reaching almost to the zipper teeth. It is extremely important that you make sure the top of the second half of the zipper is exactly in line with the first half. Put the zipper together, zip it up, and then pin the top of the second half to the top of the folded edge of the other half of the skirt. Fold the tape back as before and then unzip it to divide the halves. Fasten this side of the zipper in place along its entire length, then sew it in just as you did the other side. When the job has been completed, zip the zipper open and shut a couple of times to be sure you have put it in exactly right—this is the only way to be really sure, and it is easier to correct mistakes now than after the rest of the skirt is sewn.

Now stitch the darts in the back and the front of the skirt.

Put the two parts of each pocket together, right side to right side, and make a ½-inch seam down the straight, inside edge and across the bottom of each one. Make a similar seam on the curved edge of each pocket. So that the pocket will lie flat, you need to clip the seams for ease, as in Chapter 1. Clip the corner at the bottom of each pocket, clip toward the seam on the curved edges, and turn right side out.

Pin each pocket in place on each side of the front of the skirt. The top of the pocket should coincide with the top of the waistline of the skirt, and the short side seam of the pocket (which you left open) will be sewn into the side seam of the skirt. Pin the pockets securely in place, keeping the pins away from the edges of the waistline and the side seams so they won't be in your way when you sew. Stitch them to the skirt along the straight inside edge and across the bottom.

Pin the front and back of the skirt together, right side of material to right side, and sew the side seams ⅝ of an inch deep, stitching from top to bottom.

Your skirt is now almost finished, and this is a good time to try it on to see if you want to make any changes in it. The waistline should come ½ inch above your natural waistline. The side seams should run straight down the center of the sides of your body and should nowhere bulge or pull. Check the darts to be sure they are right—it is easy to take them out and change them at this stage.

When the skirt fits properly, you are ready to **apply an inside facing to the waistline,** which takes the place of a waistband on this skirt. From the skirt

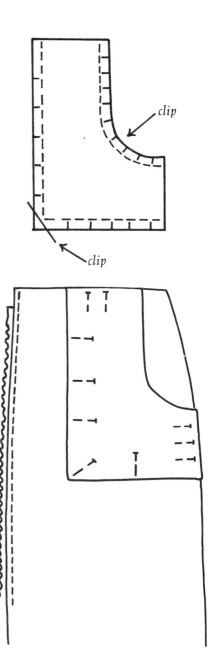

clip

clip

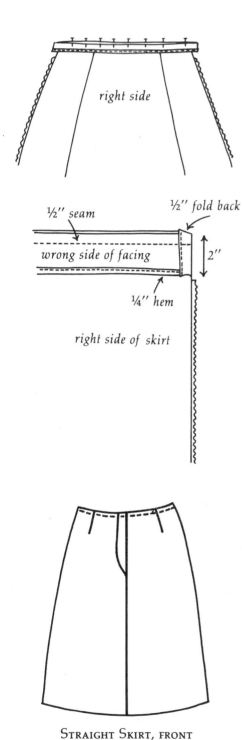

right side

½" seam   ½" fold back

wrong side of facing   2"

¼" hem

right side of skirt

STRAIGHT SKIRT, FRONT

material, cut a strip of material 1 inch longer than the waistline and 2 inches wide. Fold a ¼-inch single hem along one long edge of the facing and sew it down. Zip the skirt open, so you are working with it laid out flat, and pin the strip in place, with the unhemmed edge exactly even with the waistline of the skirt, right side of strip to right side of skirt. The strip should extend ½ inch beyond the waistline at each side of the zipper. Fold this surplus material back to match the front opening on either side and stitch down to the facing only, as shown. Stitch the facing in place around the waistline with a ½-inch seam. Fold the facing to the wrong side of the skirt along the line of stitching and sew it in place ⅛ inch below the folded edge. This line of stitching will show on the right side of the skirt. Sew the hook and eye at the top of the zipper opening.

You are now ready to hem the skirt, and here's a clever technique for **marking an even hemline.** Find a table with a top that is lower than your hip line and chalk one edge of the top heavily. Stand next to the chalked area so that it touches the skirt and turn slowly in a complete circle, making sure that the chalk marks the skirt. The chalk on the skirt will mark a straight line based on the hang of this particular skirt. Use the line as a guide for the hem, measuring down from it to the actual hemline, and you will have a straight hem. Use a standard hem with seam binding as in Chapter 4.

STRAIGHT SKIRT

Although this skirt is also based on the A-line Skirt pattern, it flares less at the sides, as its name implies, than the sports skirt. You will make a new pattern for it, and since the pattern will be useful many times in the future, you will want to make it in a suitable material for your permanent collection.

Beginning with the skirt front, put your A-line Skirt pattern on muslin or other pattern-cutting material that you have folded double so that you can cut both sides of the skirt front at once. Place the center line of the pattern 1⅞ inches away from the fold of the material. Draw around the pattern, then use a yardstick to make a straight line from the hip line to the hemline of the skirt, replacing the original slanted line. Chalk along the center line.

Cut out the pattern, and then unfold it to cut the front into unequal halves. Allow a ⅝-inch seam allowance on the left side of the center line (which will be the right-hand side of the skirt), and 1¼ inches on the right-side (which will be the left-hand side of the skirt). Chalk these seam lines; then transfer the dart markings as on page 68.

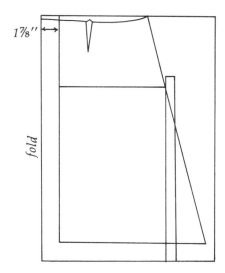

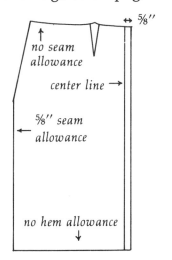

STRAIGHT SKIRT, RIGHT FRONT

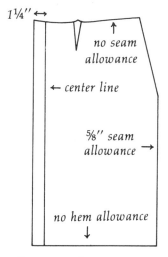

STRAIGHT SKIRT, LEFT FRONT

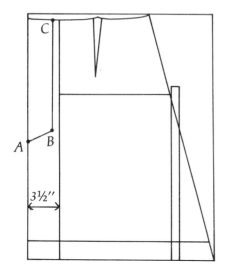

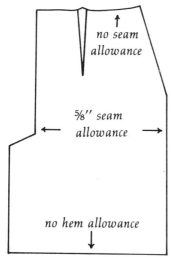

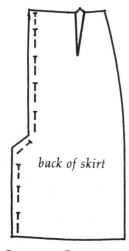

STRAIGHT SKIRT, BACK

To make the pattern for the back of the straight skirt, lay the pattern for the back of the A-line skirt on folded material with the center line of the pattern 3½ inches from the fold of the cloth. Mark a point—A— on the folded edge 5 inches below the hip line of the skirt. Mark a second point—B—4 inches below the hip line and ⅝ inch to the left of the center line of the original skirt pattern. Connect these two points with a slanted line to form a **walking pleat.** To provide seam allowance, draw a vertical line ⅝ inch to the left of the center line, connecting points B and C as shown. Then extend the bottom line of the skirt to the fold.

Adjust the side seam so that it matches the side seam of the front of the skirt, cut out the pattern, and transfer the dart markings.

You need to pin the whole pattern together in order to fit it, so begin with the back of the skirt. Pin the back seam together from the waistline to the top of the pleat allowance, then pin across the slanted line that is the top of the pleat. Next pin down the length of the pleat to the bottom of the skirt. Open the skirt with the wrong side facing you, and fold the pleat as shown. Pin the top of the pleat down flat to the skirt. On the actual skirt, these pinned seams will be sewn in place, and you can see now why this particular pleat is so successful. Folded back on the body of the skirt, it lies perfectly flat, and the folded edge is a continuation of the center seam at the back of the skirt. When you stitch the top of the pleat to the skirt, you are making an unusually strong pleat that will not pull out with use. Many skirt pleats are fastened at just one point at the top, and even if you strengthen that point with tape or embroidery, with

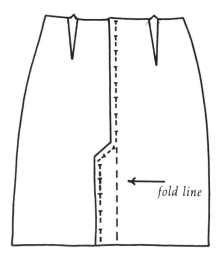

fold line

frequent use the pleat tends to pull out. No matter how much you wear this skirt, the pleat will remain intact and never look bunchy.

Pin the darts in the back of the skirt. Then pin the darts in the front of the skirt, and pin the two front sections together along the chalked seam lines. Pin the side seams and put on the skirt pattern, inside out. Fit it in the same way you did the Basic A-line Skirt pattern, checking the side seams particularly.

This skirt can be made of wool or woollike acrylic, and can be whatever length you wish. Estimate as before the amount of material required, remembering to add a ½-inch seam allowance at the waistline and 3 inches for a hem. You will also need two strips of fabric for a zipper facing, each 2 inches wide and 3½ inches longer than the zipper, a spool of matching thread, a package of seam binding, a hook and eye for the waistline, and a 7- or 9-inch skirt zipper. You will also need a strip of fabric for the waistline facing. You can use either the same fabric from which you make the skirt or commercial waistband tape. In either case, you will need a strip that is the length of the waistline plus 2½ inches. If you are using a self-facing, plan to cut it 3 inches wide.

Once you have your supplies, cut out the skirt back and fronts and transfer the markings.

The first step in completing the skirt is to finish the front placket opening. **Putting in a fly-front zipper** is really quite easy, and the results make a handsomely tailored appearance. The trick is in the use of unequal seam allowances on the front of the skirt. (If you don't tell anyone how you did it, you'll have the reputation of being a skilled tailor.)

You already have cut the fronts to allow for the

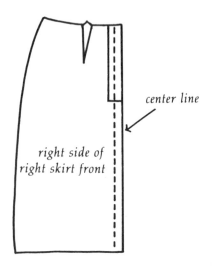

center line

right side of
right skirt front

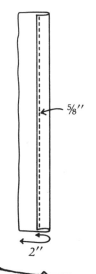

⅝″

2″

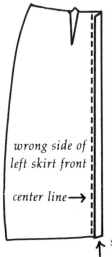

wrong side of
left skirt front

center line→

↑ ⅝″

unequal seam. Now cut two strips in the same fabric as the skirt, each 2 inches wide and 3½ inches longer than the skirt zipper. The right side of the opening should lap over the left, so lay one strip of fabric along the center line of the right-hand side of the skirt so that the edges match, right sides together. Sew with a ⅝-inch seam. This will be the side that laps over.

Put a ⅝-inch single hem down the length of the other strip of fabric. Iron down a ⅝-inch seam allowance on the left-hand side of the skirt. (You still have your chalked center line, which is 1¼ inches from the front edge of the skirt.)

On the left-hand side of the skirt, make a sandwich at the zipper opening, with the folded edge of the skirt just reaching the zipper teeth and the hemmed strip of fabric lying beneath the zipper, its unhemmed edge extending slightly beyond the zipper tape on the skirt side and the hemmed edge extending about 1½ inches on the other side. The top of the zipper should be 1½ inches down from the waistline of the skirt. Fold the top of the tape back. You can now sew this seam exactly as it is pinned. Begin at the top of the skirt and sew along the fold to the bottom of the zipper.

Working now on the right-hand side of the skirt, fold under the strip of fabric right on the line of stitches. Pin the free side of the zipper to this side of the skirt, with the folded edge extending ⅝ inch past the zipper teeth. This should be ⅝ inch past the teeth of the *entire* zipper, so zip it up to be accurate.

When the zipper is pinned securely in place, mark on this side of the skirt a spot exactly below the bottom of the zipper. When the zipper is zipped up, the

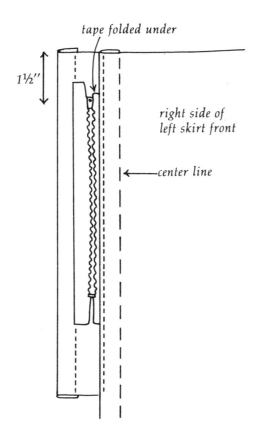

tape folded under

1½″

right side of left skirt front

center line

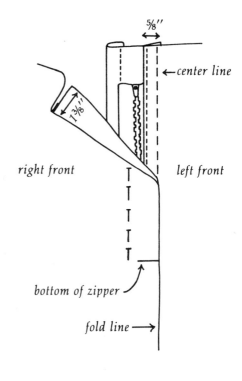

⅝″

center line

right front

1³⁄₈″

left front

bottom of zipper

fold line →

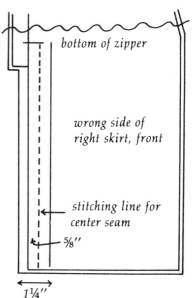

bottom of zipper

wrong side of right skirt, front

stitching line for center seam

⅝″

1¼″

folded edge of the right-hand front should be exactly at the chalked center line on the left-hand front. Unzip the zipper and sew the center seam from the marked spot to the bottom of the skirt. You will have a ⅝-inch seam allowance on the right-hand side, and a 1¼-inch seam allowance on the left-hand side, which can be trimmed off later.

Now you are ready to sew the zipper to the right-hand side of the skirt. With the zipper open, unpin it and spread the facing out flat, repinning the zipper to the *facing strip only*, in exactly the same position it

89

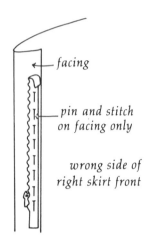

facing

pin and stitch
on facing only

wrong side of
right skirt front

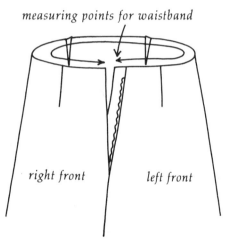

measuring points for waistband

right front   left front

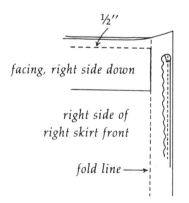

½″

facing, right side down

right side of
right skirt front

fold line →

was before. Fold the top of the zipper tape back on itself, so it slants away from the opening. Zip up the zipper and fold the facing strip back to the wrong side. Check to be sure the front of the skirt is perfectly flat along the seam line. When the zipper has been pinned correctly, stitch it to the facing.

At this point your fly-front zipper is finished except for one seam, and it is easier to finish the rest of the skirt and attach the waistband before making this final line of stitches.

Sew the darts in the front and back of the skirt, and sew the back seam of the skirt. Sew the walking pleat in place exactly as you pinned it on your pattern. Pin the side seams, then stitch them. The waistband for this skirt is an inside facing, similar to the one on the sports skirt, but it will have some modifications because of the fly-front opening. You can use either a self-facing or commercial waistband tape. Cut either one long enough to reach from the seam line on the right-hand front of the skirt to ½ inch beyond the strip of backing on the other side of the skirt.

If you are using fabric for the facing, instead of commercial tape, cut a strip 3 inches wide and fold it in half lengthwise. Pin it in place on the right side of the skirt, with the raw edge matching the raw edge of the skirt waistline. Remember to leave ½ inch of fabric extending beyond the left-hand side of the skirt. On the right-hand side, open out the strip of facing so the band is attached only to the skirt itself, not to the facing. Sew the facing on with a ½-inch seam. Fold the facing back to the wrong side on the line of stitches. On the left-hand side of the skirt, turn under the raw edge at the end. On the right-hand side, the zipper facing will fold back over the waistline facing.

As shown, fold under the top of the zipper facing to match the front of the skirt.

If you are using commercial waistband tape, fold the edge of the skirt's waistline to the wrong side, making a fold the depth of the seam allowance you added (½ inch). Pin the tape on top of the fold on the wrong side of the skirt, with the top edge of the tape ⅛ inch down from the fold. Position it exactly as you would the fabric (see above) with the tape against the skirt only, not the facing, on the right-hand side. Stitch it in place and finish the ends as with the self-facing.

Now is the time to finish the fly-front opening. There is still a raw edge on the facing on the right-hand side of the skirt. Fold this raw edge under to make a single hem. Stitch it down to the skirt front, from the waistband to ¾ inch below the bottom of the zipper, finishing with a curve that just meets the center seam. Stitch back and forth at the end of the seam to secure it.

To complete your skirt, sew around the top with a line of stitches ⅛ inch from the edge, as shown. Sew down the folded end on the left-hand side also. Sew a hook and eye at the top of the zipper opening, trim away the excess material from the seam on the left-hand side of the skirt front, and hem your skirt the same way you did the sports skirt. That's all there is to it!

In this chapter you have cut and fitted two skirt patterns based on your own measurements, and you have learned two ways of putting in a zipper; you have also learned to make the most efficient sort of skirt pleat there is. Now you are ready to tackle a new and entirely different project.

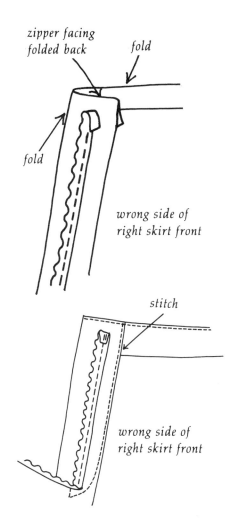

zipper facing folded back

fold

fold

wrong side of right skirt front

stitch

wrong side of right skirt front

· 7 ·

Putting in a Lining:
A Warm Robe

The best way to master a new sewing technique is to make one or two garments that require the use of the technique. In this way you not only learn something new; you increase your skills and your wardrobe at one and the same time. The new technique in this case is putting a lining into a garment; the project is a warm robe.

There are a number of reasons why garments need to be lined. Often, like the robe in question, it is because the materials used are rough and scratchy on the inside. Adding a lining of smooth material will make them more comfortable. Often, too, a lining is added for warmth. Garments made of very sheer, transparent cloth are frequently lined to add weight and body to the garment, so it will hang better, and for the sake of appearance. Some garments are lined to help them hold their shape—many skirts, for instance, have a half-lining from the waistline to below the hips to keep the material from stretching when the skirt is worn.

ROBE

The robe is similar in construction to the peasant blouse (see Chapter 1) in that it, too, is made from rectangles, but its dimensions are different. You can use plush, fake fur, or corduroy, all napped fabrics that require a special fabric layout.

It is best to make a cloth pattern using scrap material, so that you can fit it properly. If you can find an old pair of draperies, a medium-heavy bedspread, or something similar in weight, it will enable you to judge how the heavy material of the robe itself will look.

The body of the robe is made of two matching rectangles—one for the front and one for the back—cut 12 inches wider than the width of your shoulders and 3 inches longer than the finished robe will be. The sleeves are also matching rectangles, 20 inches each in width, including ⅝-inch seams. To get their length, measure from the top of your arm to the length you want the sleeves to be, and then, because the robe has dropped shoulders, subtract 4 inches. The final figure for the length of the sleeves includes 1 inch for a hem at the bottom and a ⅝-inch seam allowance.

Cut out the pattern pieces in these dimensions. Cut the rectangle for the front of the robe in half lengthwise. Put the two sections together, and using your pattern for a fitted neckline (see Chapter 2),

93

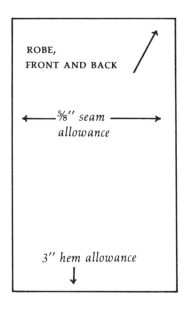

ROBE, FRONT AND BACK

⅝" seam allowance

3" hem allowance

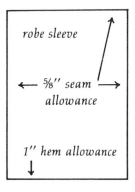

robe sleeve

⅝" seam allowance

1" hem allowance

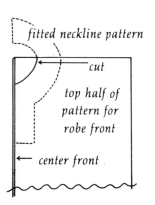

fitted neckline pattern

cut

top half of pattern for robe front

center front

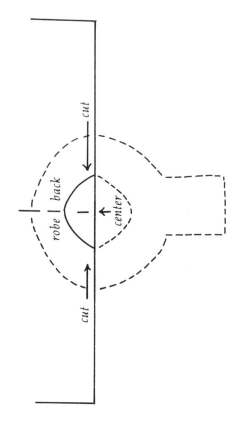

round off the points at the center front. Use the same neckline pattern to cut the back neckline. Pin all the pattern pieces together with ⅝-inch seams, pinning the shoulder seams first, then pinning the sleeves to the body as you did on the peasant blouse in Chapter 1. Pin the side and sleeve seams and try the pattern on to make sure that the body of the robe is not too wide and the sleeves are the right length. The finished robe is deliberately bulky in appearance (thus making use of one of the characteristics of the material), and it must be wide enough for the two front pieces to lap over slightly below the neckline. The sleeves should not be so wide that they will be uncomfortable to wear, and they can be any length you wish.

The robe has a 2-inch-wide tie belt that is similar to the sash in Chapter 1 and can be made in one of several ways. Unless the fabric is too stiff and bulky, you can make the belt from the same material as the robe, or you can use some of the lining material unless it is too flimsy to hold its shape. In any case you will need a strip of material 5 inches wide and the necessary length plus 1 inch for hems. To find the length, wrap a string once around your waist, tie it in a bow or a loose knot, cut off the ends at whatever length you like, and measure the string. You can also use both robe and lining material, with the latter lining the belt just as it does the robe. In this case, you will need two strips of material, each 3 inches wide and the necessary length plus 1 inch for hems.

Once your pattern has been perfected, you are ready to estimate the amount of material you must buy for the robe. You will need the same amount of lining material, as well as a spool of matching thread and enough seam binding for the bottom hems of both robe and lining.

When shopping for materials for your robe and lining, think of them as a combination. This pattern has a completely different finished appearance depending upon the fabrics of which it is made. You can use regular dress lining material for the lining, or any lightweight material that pleases you. The two requirements for the lining are that it be made of a color that harmonizes with the robe and that it be opaque enough to hide the inside seams.

A robe of navy-blue corduroy with a striped red-and-white lining would look rather tailored; a robe of black plush lined with lipstick-red dress lining would look elegant; and a robe of gold fake fur lined with pale-green crepe would look feminine. A good way to make your choice is to select the robe material first, then put various possible lining materials next to it until you find the perfect combination. You will notice an interesting thing when you match up fabrics in this way, which is that colors vary greatly in different fabrics because of the type of dye used and the nature of the fabric. Normally, navy blue goes well with red and white, but sometimes when you put materials of these colors together, they clash instead of complementing each other. Certain other combinations of colors in specific materials actually seem to light up and look more beautiful together than either does alone. This is the reason for checking the robe and lining material together before making your purchase.

Napped fabrics have a peculiar characteristic that must be taken into account when they are used. They have what is called an "up" and a "down" appear-

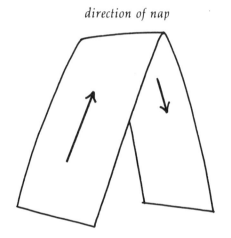

direction of nap

ance, and all pattern pieces must be cut with this in mind. If you make a garment with the front "up" of the nap and the sleeves "down," the pieces will look as if they were cut from different materials when sewn together. This peculiarity does not show when the material is laid out flat to be cut, so it is necessary to chalk the direction of the nap on the material before cutting. You can make chalked rows of arrows down the entire length of fabric, or you can keep this principle in mind while laying out the pattern pieces, and mark the top of each piece with a chalked T. Because of the nap, you must cut the back and front of the robe separately. If you cut them in one piece, to be folded at the shoulder line, the nap of the back would go one way and the nap of the front the other.

Before cutting the material, it is a good idea to test both robe and lining fabrics to learn how the completed robe must be cleaned. Many fake furs and plushes are washable, as are many lining and other lightweight fabrics. If you know this to be the case with the materials you've selected, you can toss the robe right into the laundry with no qualms, but if you suspect your materials should not go into a washing machine or drier, now is the time to find out.

To test a fabric for washability, cut a small irregularly shaped piece of the material and draw around its outline on a sheet of paper. Label the drawing to indicate what fabric it represents. Pin a large safety pin through the piece of material and put it through the regular wash cycle of your machine. Take it out of the washer (the safety pin will make it easy to find), stretch it out flat, and lay it on top of your drawing. If its outline matches the drawing perfectly, then you know the fabric can go through your normal washing cycle. If it has shrunk very much, you may want to try another sample with a short-time cool-water wash to see if it will take that without shrinkage.

Some materials wash perfectly in any wash cycle, but shrink or become twisted out of shape in the drier. Because of this, put your sample of wet material in the drier and see what happens to it there.

You may find that the material for your robe, and/or the lining, can be washed in a regular cycle, but cannot go through the drier. You may find that they can be washed in a shorter cooler cycle but cannot go in the drier. You may find they take both processes perfectly well. Whatever you discover, make a note of it, so that you will later know how to care for your robe.

Cut out the body of the robe, both front and back, remembering to mark the top of each piece with chalk. Cut the front in half down the center line. Cut both sleeves, remembering to mark the top of each. Then adapt the neckline on each side of the front of the robe to give it a modified kimono slant, just as you did for the Happi coat in Chapter 2.

Cut the lining to match the pieces of the robe exactly.

Baste the shoulders of the robe together, and baste the sleeves to the body of the robe. Pin the side and sleeve seams and try on the robe. Lap the right side of the robe over the left, and use a string or piece of yarn as a substitute belt to tie around your waist. Check the appearance of the robe in the mirror, noting whether it has the right dimensions for you. The robe material may look quite different from the material

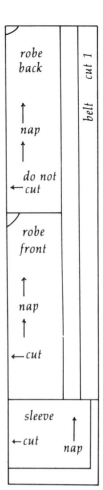

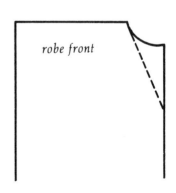

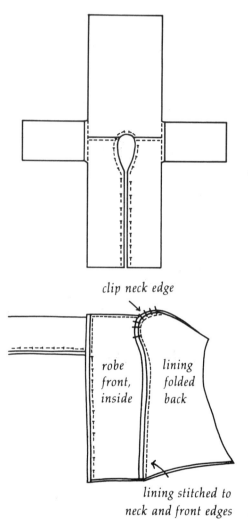

clip neck edge

robe front, inside | lining folded back

lining stitched to neck and front edges

you used to cut a sample pattern, so make adjustments if necessary. Then, using the robe as a guide, change the lining in exactly the same way. Sew together the shoulder seams of the robe and sew the sleeves to the body, but leave the sleeve and side seams open.

Sew the lining together in the same way as the robe. Lay the robe out flat right side up on a table or the floor and put the lining on top of it, right side down.

Pin the robe and the lining together. Begin pinning at the bottom of the neckline and go down one side. Do the same on the other side. Then pin around the neckline. Sew these seams ⅝ inch deep, doing them in the same order in which you pinned. Clip around the neckline to ease the seam (see page 11). Separate the body of the robe from the lining and match the side and sleeve seams of the robe. Begin pinning at the underarm point and pin from there to the ends of the sleeves and the bottom of the robe. Sew as you pinned, making ⅝-inch seams. Do the same to the lining.

Now turn the robe right side out, with the lining inside. Put the lining sleeves inside the robe sleeves. Make sure the lining and robe are even all the way around the front opening. The lining should not show on the outside of the robe, and the robe material should not show on the wrong side. Press well or pin around the front opening to hold this seam in place.

Your fully lined robe is almost finished. There are only two more steps to complete: putting the hems in the robe and lining and making a tie belt. Starting at the underarm point, pin the robe and lining to-gether. Pin along the sleeve seams toward the ends of the sleeve and along the side seams to the bottom of the robe, stopping 3 inches before the end of each. The purpose of this pinning is to hold the two layers together while you do the hems. Try the robe on again to make a final check of sleeve and robe lengths. Mark the desired lengths on the bottom of the robe on one side of the front opening, and on one sleeve. Remove the robe and match the sleeves so they will be the same length, marking the end of the second sleeve with a pin.

Put the robe on a hanger, suspend it in a doorway where it can hang freely, and leave it overnight. This allows the material to settle into shape, so that your hems will be even. If you hemmed the robe be-forehand, the "settling" process, which occurs in all heavy materials, might so change the way the robe hangs that you would have to rehem it.

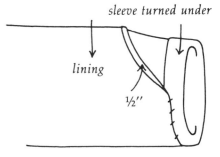

sleeve turned under

lining

½"

To finish the ends of the sleeves, fold the outside fabric of each sleeve under at the desired length and pin. Turn the robe wrong side out and turn the lining under so that the edge of the lining comes ½ inch from the end of the sleeve. Sew the lining to the robe, using invisible stitches.

Put the robe on a hanger to pin the bottom hem. Fold the bottom of the robe to the desired length, pinning it every three inches. (Stop occasionally to check the length of the garment, matching side seams, front opening, and back of robe against each other.) Turn the robe wrong side out and pin up the hem in the lining to match the one in the robe. When you have finished, the bottom of the robe should

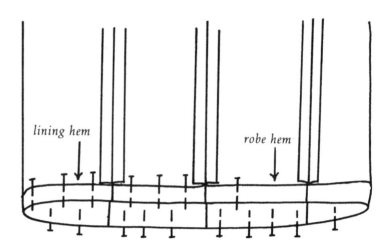

lining hem   robe hem

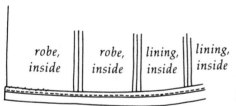

robe, inside   robe, inside   lining, inside   lining, inside

hang in a straight line, with the lining matching it exactly. Trim the raw edges of the hems so that they are the same depth all around. Press or pin the hem in place.

Remove the pins, spread the robe and lining apart, and sew the seam binding in a continuous line all around the bottom of the robe and lining, wrong side of binding to right side of hem. Fold the hem in place and sew the other edge of the binding to the robe and lining, using invisible stitches.

A **tie belt** is made like a doubled sash, but is narrower. Because it is narrow, it is difficult to turn right side out after it is sewn—unless you know a certain trick.

If you are making the belt from either the robe material or the lining material, fold the single strip in half lengthwise, right sides together. Now for the trick. Before sewing the long side seam, cut a length of string or strong yarn a few inches longer than the belt and put it inside the folded material, with one end lying across the beginning of the seam line,

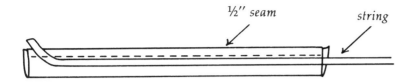

½" seam   string

where it will be sewn into the seam. Pin the long sides together, and then sew, making a ½-inch seam and catching the string into the beginning of the seam. When the seam is finished, push the end of the belt where the string is sewn into the seam down inside the tube. Pull gently on the end of the string at the other end of the tube to turn the belt right side out. Clip off the string, fold the raw edges inside ½ inch at both ends of the belt, and stitch by hand.

To make a lined belt, lay one strip on top of the other, right side to right side, and pin along both sides. Put the length of string between the two pieces of material with one end lying across the end of one side seam. Proceed as before, making a ½-inch seam on each side and catching the string into the beginning of one of them.

Put the robe on, tie the belt around your waist, and see what a wonderful addition to your wardrobe you have made—at a fraction of the cost of buying it!

· 8 ·

Two Shirt Dresses: One Basic, One Feminine

If there is a single dress style that is always in vogue, it is the shirt dress. Every pattern collection should include this classic. It looks good on almost everyone and can be adapted for wear on almost any occasion.

The distinctive features of the shirt dress are a tailored collar and a buttoned front opening; beyond that, there are unlimited variations. The ultimate model has pockets with flaps, a back yoke, long cuffed sleeves, and other characteristics of the shirt which give it its name, but whether or not yours will have any or all of these is a matter of personal preference. You can start with a basic design, with a zipper up the front, and then create all the variations you like.

BASIC SHIRT DRESS

Begin by getting out your Basic A-line Dress pattern. Prepare enough newspaper for a dress-length pattern and place the front of your A-line Dress pattern on it so that the center front is 1½ inches from the left-hand edge of the newspaper.

Draw around the neckline, extending the line to the left-hand edge of the newspaper. Draw down the shoulder seam. An armhole for a dress with fitted sleeves should be slightly larger than for a sleeveless dress, so you will need to increase the size of the armhole on your pattern. (The reason for this is that a sleeveless dress allows lots of free arm movement whereas a sleeve may restrict it a bit.) To enlarge the armhole, move the side seam of the dress out ½ inch and extend the regular armhole to that point. Curve the side seam slightly to extend it, as shown. Now add ⅝-inch seam allowance all around the armhole.

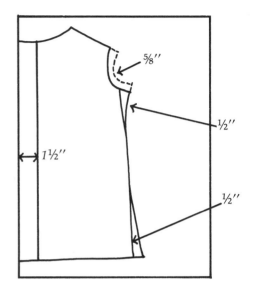

You can copy the rest of the side seam from your A-line Dress pattern, or you may wish to modify it slightly. The skirt of a shirt dress generally has a straight appearance, so you may wish to elimi-nate some of the flare. Don't make the skirt too tight, however; you need to be able to move comfortably.

Make the pattern for the back of the dress in the same way, but do not add extra material at the center back.

You are now going to take the stupendous step of cutting a sleeve pattern to fit the armhole of your dress. Like all other sewing techniques, this is not nearly as difficult as it seems.

The drawing shows a typical pattern for a **fitted short sleeve,** designed from average measurements. Although it may not fit you precisely, it will give you a basis with which to work. Make graph paper by marking off newspaper in one-inch squares, and fol-lowing the directions in Chapter 3 for graphing pat-

1 square = 1″

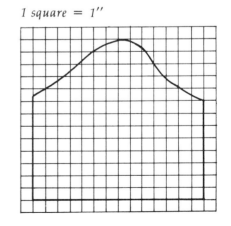

103

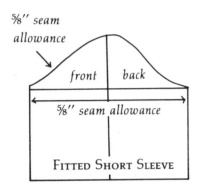

front | back

⅝″ seam allowance

FITTED SHORT SLEEVE

terns, duplicate the sleeve pattern on the graph paper. You will notice that the sleeve pattern, when folded double, has a deeper curve on one side—the back side—than on the other. This is to allow extra room for arm movement. Mark the front side of the pattern—the one with the more shallow curve—F, so you will be sure to put the sleeves into the dress correctly. The pattern includes a ⅝-inch seam allowance at the top and sides.

When the sleeve pattern has been cut, measure around its armhole and the armhole of the dress pattern. The sleeve armhole should be ⅝ inch larger than that of the dress; the extra amount is to be eased into the seam for a better fit.

If your sleeve pattern needs to be made larger at the armhole, spread out the pattern, and make six 3-inch slashes 1½ inches apart on the top edge; lay the sleeve out flat on a piece of paper, spread apart the slashed openings to increase the size of the armhole line, and draw around the top edge to make a new armhole. To make the sleeve smaller, cut the same number and size of slashes into the pattern, but overlap the pieces. Copy the remainder of the new sleeve from the original pattern. If you find that the armhole is still not large enough, add a small amount to each end of the sleeve, as shown.

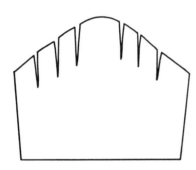

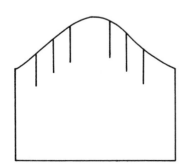

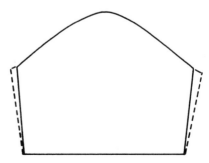

Now cut out a cloth pattern of the back, the front, and sleeves of the dress from muslin or other pattern-cutting material. Fold the front of the dress in half lengthwise, and cut it in half along the fold.

Pin the shoulder seams together. Then pin the two halves of the front of the dress, making a seam 1½ inches wide, but leaving it unpinned the top 9 inches. (This takes up the extra material you allowed for the front opening.) Fold one of the sleeves in half lengthwise and match the fold to the shoulder seam of the dress. With the sleeve and dress still flat (not sewn into tubes) pin the sleeve in place, right sides together, easing the extra ⅝ inch into the armhole. Since you are dealing with two bias edges of material, this can be easily done. To aid the process, you can first run a line of gathering stitches around the top of the sleeve. Use long stitches and begin and end the stitches two inches from the underarm seams. Repeat with the other sleeve. You need both sleeves in place in order to fit the dress properly.

When the sleeves have been pinned in the dress, pin the sleeve seams and side seams of the dress, beginning at the underarm point and continuing from there to the end of the sleeve and to the bottom of the dress pattern. Slip on the dress pattern inside out and stand in front of a mirror.

First check the armhole seams. On top, these should come just at the points of your shoulders, and neither above nor below it. If they are not right, adjust them. Let your arms hang straight down at your sides and see if the material of the front of the dress bulges in front of your arm on either side. If it does, repin the sleeves to take up excess material from the dress. Now move your arms back as far as they will

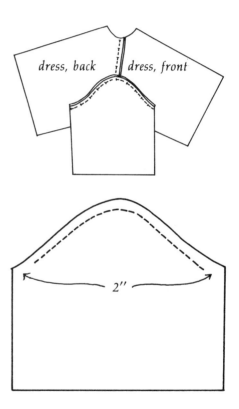

dress, back   dress, front

2"

go. The fit of the sleeves and armholes must be loose enough for easy movement, but not so loose as to be sloppy-looking.

Either have a friend help you adjust the back of the armholes and sleeves, or set up a mirror so that you can see your back plainly. Let your arms hang down by your sides and see if there are any extra bulges or wrinkles either in the sleeves or in the back of the dress. If so, adjust the seams as you did before, and then move your arms forward to see if you have taken up too much material. When you think you have both the front and the back of the armhole seams properly adjusted, move your arms around in all directions to see if you have allowed yourself enough room. It's said that there used to be stars in Hollywood who had their dresses fitted so tightly that the ladies had to be sewn into them, but they also had to be picked up and carried when they moved from place to place because they couldn't walk. What you are aiming for is to have both a good fit and a comfortable dress. Decide on the sleeve length you want and adjust your pattern. It is easiest to decide on the length if you make the sleeves without hem allowance.

Check the side seams of the pattern to see how they look. This dress should fit fairly smoothly over the hips, but not so tightly that it bulges in front or sags under the buttocks in an ugly way. When you adjust the side seams at any one point, adjust the whole seam for a smooth appearance.

If you find this fitting tedious and difficult, try an experiment. Put on a commercially made dress that you feel is an excellent fit and look at yourself in the mirror to check the armholes and side seams. You may find that the dress is not such a perfect fit as you thought. This is why it is worthwhile to take the necessary time to make a well-fitting pattern.

Next test the width of the skirt for ease in walking. If you have decided on a rather snug fit, you may need to add a pleat in the back to allow you to walk comfortably. The walking pleat that you used in the straight skirt can be used in the back of the shirt dress. Turn to Chapter 6 and change the pattern for the back of the dress to include the pleat.

When your patterns suit you, label and mark them carefully, including "no seam allowance" at the neckline of the dress. Now you can estimate how much material you will need. Include in your estimate 2½ inches for hem allowance on the dress and 2 inches on the sleeves. Before purchasing a zipper, remember what you read in Chapter 6. If your pattern is snugly fitted, you may need a zipper that extends just below the hip line. If it is not, you will need one that extends only far enough to allow you to put the dress on easily over your head. The color of the zipper should match the dress. You will also need a spool of matching thread and a snap fastener for the neckline.

When you are ready to cut the dress, fold the dress front pattern in half, lay it on a fold of material, and cut it out. Remember to add ½ inch at the neckline and 2½ inches for the hem. Before unfolding the material, chalk the center line along its entire length on the right side of the material.

The front of the dress will have a lapped opening for the zipper, that is, one that laps over from the right to the left side of the dress, so you will need more material on the right side of the front than on

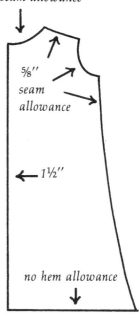

SHIRT DRESS, FRONT

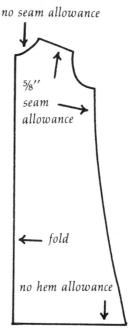

SHIRT DRESS, BACK

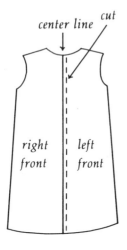

center line · cut

right front | left front

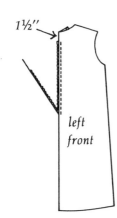

1½″

left front

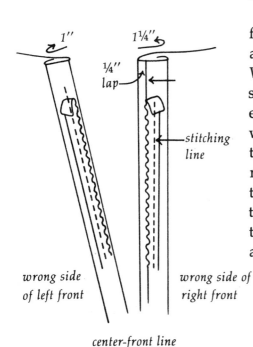

1″ · 1¼″

¼″ lap

stitching line

wrong side of left front

wrong side of right front

center-front line

the left. Cut the front opening 1 inch to the right of the chalked center line, which will give you 2 inches of extra material on the right-hand side of the dress, and 1 inch of extra material on the left.

Cut out the back of the dress and the sleeves, adding seam and hem allowances where necessary, and prepare to put a **lapped zipper** in the front. This is sewn in in exactly the same way as the fly-front zipper in Chapter 6, except that the bottom of the zipper opening is finished differently.

Fold the left-hand side of the front of the dress under ¼ inch and stitch down. (This is to make an edge that will not ravel when you use the zipper.) Now fold this edge under ¾ of an inch (which uses up the 1 inch on this side) and put the unzipped zipper under the fold, so that the fold just reaches the teeth of the zipper. Set the top of the zipper 1½ inches down from the bottom of the neckline, fold under the tape at the top of the zipper, pin the zipper in place along its entire length, and stitch.

The line chalked on the right-hand side of the dress front marks the exact center of the front of the dress, and this line is to come exactly over the zipper teeth. Working with this section of the dress on the wrong side, fold the edge back 1¼ inches, then fold the raw edge under ¼ inch. Put the zipper on top of this fold with the teeth facing down, placing the zipper so that the teeth are exactly under the chalked line on the right side of the material. Pin the zipper in place at the top, then close it to make sure that on both sides the zipper is the same distance from the neckline of the dress. When both sides are even, pin the zipper all the way to the bottom, unzip it, and stitch in place on the wrong side of the dress, sewing through both thicknesses of material.

Turn the dress front to the right side and mark the bottom of the zipper with chalk. (You can feel it through the material.) Starting just below the zipper, fold the rest of the right-hand side of the dress over the left, so that it laps over the same distance along the zipper opening. Pin.

Starting at the bottom of the row of stitches you just made—those that hold the zipper in place on the right-hand side of the dress—sew across the bottom of the zipper in a slanted line to the edge of the lapped fold and then sew down the edge of the lapped fold to the bottom of the dress.

That is the way to make a lapped zipper closing, and now you know the three basic ways of putting a zipper in a garment: in-seam, fly-front, and lapped.

If your dress has a back pleat, sew it in place as you did on the straight skirt in Chapter 6. Finish the back seam, and sew the shoulder seams of the dress.

You are now ready to sew the sleeves in the dress. Run a line of gathering stitches over the tops of the sleeves, as you did with the pattern. Fold one sleeve in half lengthwise, and match the fold to one of the shoulder seams on the dress. Pin the rest of the sleeve in place and sew, easing the curve of the sleeve into the curve of the armhole. Be sure not to stretch the material of either, as this will show on the finished garment. If you don't get it right the first time, rip it out and do it again. Putting a sleeve into an armhole properly is the kind of skill that you learn by doing, and once you have mastered it, you will never forget it.

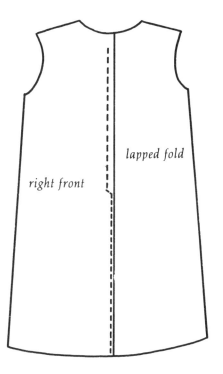

lapped fold

right front

It is now time to make the shirt collar for the dress, which is to be the same as the one you made for the tennis shirt in Chapter 3. Get out your pattern, cut out the collar, and sew it in place just as before.

If you want pockets on your dress, now is the time to add them. It is much easier to set pockets in the right position while the dress is still a flat piece of material, and much, much easier to sew them in place then. The regular shirt pocket with flap, described in Chapter 5, is right for this dress, and you may want more than one. The drawings show some typical ways to use pockets on shirt dresses.

Sew the side seams and underarm sleeve seams of the dress, following the procedure for sewing all side and sleeve seams. You may either hem the ends of the sleeves by hand, or finish them with outside facings that come to a point at the top of the sleeve to match the point of the pocket and its cuff. To do the latter, first cut 1½ inches of the hem allowance off the sleeve. Cut the facing 4 inches wide and long enough to go around the bottom opening of each sleeve, plus 1 inch for the seam. Fold the strip in half crosswise and mark a point as shown. Draw a slanting line from there to the top of the center fold, as you did with the pocket. Then cut along the line.

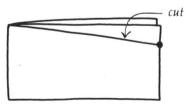

Fold the strip in half crosswise, wrong side out, and match it to the end of the sleeve. Sew a seam across the open ends to make it into a tube that will fit exactly on the end of the sleeve. Turn the sleeve wrong side out and lay the facing around the sleeve, straight edge of the facing at the end of the sleeve, right side of facing to wrong side of sleeve, seams of each matching. Sew the facing in place with a ½-inch seam. Turn the sleeve right side out, and fold the pointed facing back over the right side of the sleeve. Turn the raw edge of the facing under, pin in place, and sew the facing down to the dress.

A spaghetti strip belt looks attractive with this dress. A **spaghetti strip** is a tube of material that is filled with cording and is thus round like a piece of spaghetti. Once you have learned to make such a strip, you will want to try different varieties for various purposes. A spaghetti strip can be any diameter you wish, depending on the size of the cording you use to fill it.

To make the spaghetti strip by a foolproof and simple method, you will use the same procedure as in Chapter 7 when sewing a string inside a tube to turn the tube right side out. In this case, however, when the string pulls the fabric tube right side out, it pulls along the cording inside the tube so that when the belt is right side out, it is stuffed.

To make the strip, measure to see how long you wish your belt to be, and cut a strip that long and 1½ inches wide. Use ½-inch cording to stuff it. Fold the fabric in half lengthwise, inside out, and place a piece of string longer than the strip inside the fold, so that one end lies across the beginning of what will be the lengthwise seam line. Cut a piece of cording a few inches longer than the strip, and

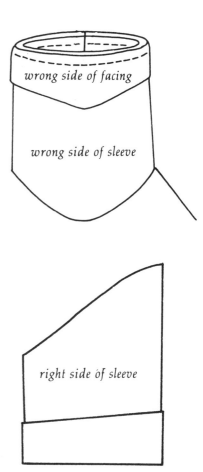

wrong side of facing

wrong side of sleeve

right side of sleeve

place one end of it across what will be the same seam line just above the string. The rest of the cording should be outside the tube, as shown. Pin the raw edges together carefully, then sew along the entire length of the strip in a ¼-inch seam, catching the string and the cording into the beginning of the seam. When the seam is finished, push the end of the belt where the string and cording are sewn into the seam down inside the tube several inches. Pull gently on the end of the string at the other end of the tube to turn the belt right side out. The cording will be pulled inside the tube. Clip off the string, fold the raw edges inside ½ inch at both ends of the belt, and stitch by hand.

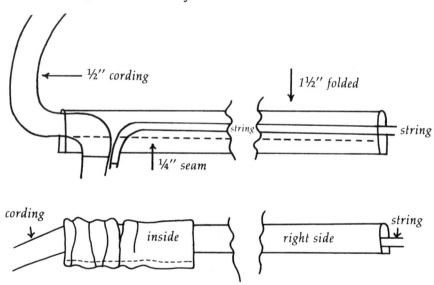

Belt loops are especially handy on a dress with a matching belt, and are easy to make. Cut two strips of material, each 4 inches long and 1 inch wide. Fold each strip in half lengthwise, and then fold the raw edges inside to make a strip ¼ inch wide. Stitch along the folds. Make each strip into a circle overlapping the ends, and stitch in place on the side seam at the waistline, sewing over and over the lapped ends.

Hem the dress, using a standard hem (see Chapter 1), and sew in place the snap at the neckline. Put the dress on, and look at yourself in the mirror!

FEMININE SHIRT DRESS

Another version of the shirt dress, which is more feminine, has long, full sleeves and a gathered skirt. You can quite easily adapt your basic pattern to make this version.

Begin with your Fitted Short Sleeve pattern, which is to be adjusted to make the pattern for a **fitted long full sleeve.** Put the pattern on a sheet of newspaper with the top 1½ inches down from the top of the paper. Measure the length of your arm from the point of your shoulder to your wrist to get the right length for this type of sleeve. (Don't forget to add the figure to your Chart of Measurements.) Add 1 inch and mark a point that distance from the top of the sleeve pattern. Draw a line through the point across the bottom of the paper.

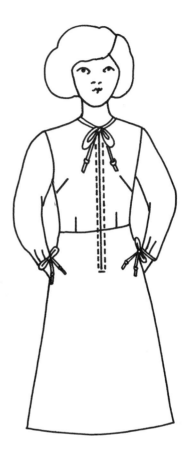

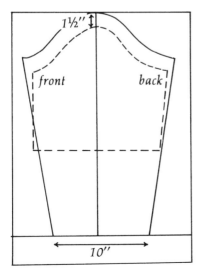

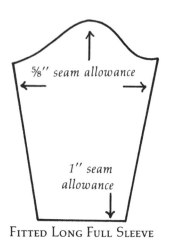

FITTED LONG FULL SLEEVE

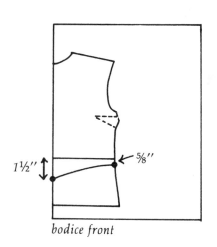

bodice front

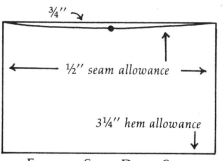

FEMININE SHIRT DRESS, SKIRT

With chalk or crayon, draw a new armhole line for the sleeve 1½ inches above the one on the pattern and extending an inch beyond it on each side. This increases the size of the armhole without changing its basic curves.

Remove the Fitted Short Sleeve pattern from the paper, and find the center of the new armhole line, marking it with a point. Draw a line through this point from the top of the armhole down to the line you drew representing the length of the sleeve. Now, using as a center the point where these two lines meet, draw a horizontal line 10 inches long to represent the end of the sleeve. With a yardstick, draw the sides of the new sleeve pattern by connecting the ends of the armhole line with the corresponding ends of the bottom line of the sleeve. Your pattern will now look like the one shown in the drawing. Label and mark it for your collection.

For the bodice of the dress, get out your pattern for the fitted blouse with darts (see Chapter 5). Fold the front of the pattern in half, lengthwise, lay it on newspaper, and draw around it. The side seam should end ⅝ inch below the waistline and the center line 1½ inches below the waistline. Take the pattern off the paper, and make a new waistline by drawing a gently curving line between these two points. Do the same with the back of the blouse pattern.

For the skirt pattern, cut a rectangle of muslin or other pattern-cutting material 1½ times as wide as your hip measurement, plus 3 inches, and 3¾ inches longer than the finished length of the skirt. Cut the rectangle in half lengthwise. Shape the waistline on each piece as you did the waistline of the bodice, drawing a gently curving line from the sides toward the center. The line should be ¾ inch lower at the center than at the sides. Label the skirt patterns and mark them "½-inch seam allowance" at the top and sides and "3¼-inch hem allowance" at the bottom.

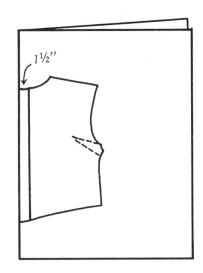

These are the main parts of the pattern for a shirt dress with full sleeves and a gathered skirt—front and back of bodice, skirt, and sleeves. Since the bodice will require further fitting, you now need to cut it out of cloth. The bodice has to fit closely around the waistline to be used as the top of a two-piece dress.

Place the newspaper pattern for the front of the bodice on a piece of folded muslin, with the center line of the pattern 1½ inches away from the fold. Extend the neckline and bottom line to the fold. Cut out the cloth bodice and cut it in half through the fold line. Transfer the dart markings from the Fitted Blouse pattern to the new bodice pattern as on page 68. Pin the darts in place. Pin the fronts together with a 1½-inch seam, leaving a large enough opening at the neckline to get the pattern over your head. Cut the back of the bodice from cloth.

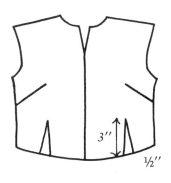

Pin the shoulder seams of the bodice, and slip it on, inside out. Mark the high point of the bust line on each side. Take off the bodice and pin two short darts in the waistline, each below the high point of the bust on that side, about ½ inch wide at the base and 3 inches long. On the back of the bodice, pin two longer waistline darts, each 2½ inches from the center line, ¾ inch wide at the base and 4 inches long.

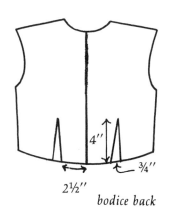

bodice back

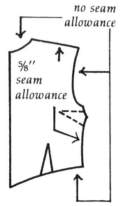

*no seam
allowance*

⅝″
*seam
allowance*

FEMININE SHIRT DRESS, BODICE FRONT

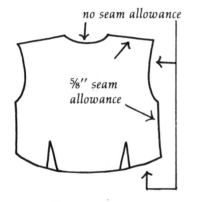

no seam allowance

⅝″ *seam
allowance*

FEMININE SHIRT DRESS, BODICE BACK

Slip the bodice pattern on again and pin the side seams at the waistline, making the pattern fit snugly. Continue pinning up to the bottom of the armholes, and then check your appearance in the mirror. Adjust the darts and the side seams until the bodice fits smoothly. Use half of the bodice front and the complete back as permanent patterns, marking the darts as on page 68. Label and mark the pattern for your collection.

Estimate how much material you will need, taking into account the fact that the sleeves must be cut the same way on the material as the rest of the pattern pieces. This dress would look good in a thin, crisp material, such as lawn or permanent-press organdy. You will need a spool of matching thread, a snap fastener, and a matching zipper long enough to reach from 1½ inches below your neckline to just below your hip line.

You don't need too many instructions for assembling this dress, since you have already learned all the techniques required.

Cut out the pieces of the dress. Sew the side and waistline darts in the front two sections of the bodice and the waistline darts in the back of the bodice, and then cut the front of the skirt in half lengthwise. Gather each half to fit the waistline of its matching bodice half, starting the gathers 2 inches from the center edge of each. (See Chapter 4 if you need directions on gathering.) Sew the fronts of the skirt to the fronts of the bodice, right sides together.

You will use an in-seam zipper in this dress. Turn the center edge of each side of the bodice-skirt combination under ½ inch from neckline to hem and stitch down. Then fold each side back 1 inch. Set the zipper in place between the two halves, and mark the point where it ends with chalk. Stitch the front of the dress closed from that point to the bottom in a straight seam. Press the seam open.

Repin the zipper in place and sew, following the same procedure as for the sports skirt in Chapter 6. However, if you prefer you can make this a concealed in-seam zipper. Place the zipper, so that the teeth are covered by the folded edges on each side. Bring the two sides together so they meet over the zipper teeth, pin the zipper in place, unzip it, and sew down each side of the zipper to the bottom. Your stitching lines will be about ¼ inch from each folded edge. Sew across the bottom of the zipper as shown.

Gather the skirt back to match the bodice back, and sew the two together. Sew the shoulder seams.

Gather the armholes of the sleeves to match the armholes of the bodice. Begin and end the stitches 2 inches from the edges and spread the gathers evenly. Then stitch down to hold them in place. Set the gathered sleeves in just as you did the plain sleeves in the basic shirt dress.

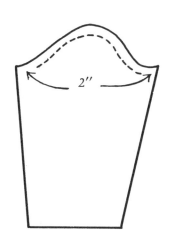

Pin the side seams of the dress, matching them at the underarm points and at the waistline. (If you've made a slight error in sewing previous seams, you can correct it at this point, so the garment pieces will match properly.) When pinning the sleeve seams, leave them open 4 inches from the end to make a placket opening so the sleeves will go easily over your hands. When the pinning is complete, sew the side and sleeve seams.

Unlike some shirt dresses, this one does not have a

117

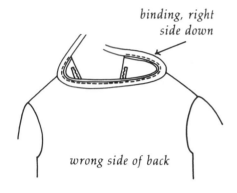

binding, right
side down

wrong side of back

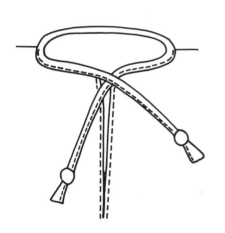

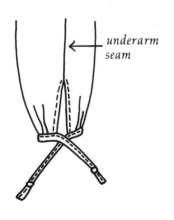

underarm
seam

tailored collar. Instead the neckline is finished with **narrow binding and tie.** That is, the neckline is bound with a straight strip of material, the ends of which are then stitched down to make a tie. Cut a strip of material 1 inch wide and 15 inches longer than the neck opening. Fold it in half crosswise and center the fold at the center back of the neckline. Pin in place, right side of strip against wrong side of dress, with one edge even with the top of the neckline. Begin pinning at the center back and continue around the rest of the neckline, then sew the strip around the neckline with a ½-inch seam as you would a regular binding. Fold the strip over to the right side of the neckline and turn the raw edge under just over the first row of stitches. Sew in place around the neckline. Fold under the two ends of the binding the same amount as the binding on the neckline and stitch down. Tie a small knot in the exact end of each tie. This neckline finish is a combination binding and tie.

The ends of the sleeves are finished in the same way. On each sleeve, fold a hem in the seam allowance on each side of the opening and stitch in place. Gather the ends of the sleeves to fit snugly around your wrist, smooth the gathers, and stitch to hold them in place. Cut a strip of binding for each sleeve end, 1½ inches wide and long enough to go around the gathered end of the sleeves plus 15 inches. Bind the sleeve ends just as you bound the neckline and stitch the rest of the binding down flat as before.

Try on your dress, mark the hemline, put in a standard hem as in Chapter 1, and your new creation is ready to wear.

· 9 ·

Three More Skirts:
Two Circle Skirts
and a Wraparound

CIRCLE SKIRT
FROM A TABLECLOTH

It's a good idea to try something really unusual in sewing from time to time, just to remind yourself how much fun experimenting can be. A popular skirt that never goes out of style and that can be made in a number of different lengths for various occasions is the circle skirt, which is actually just a complete circle of material with a waistline cut in the center. You can make one in a jiffy by buying a circular tablecloth, in a color and pattern you like, and providing it with a waistband.

Before rushing right out to buy a tablecloth, you need to learn something about taking measurements for a circular skirt. When you have grasped this, you can look at the size printed on the tag on a round tablecloth and know how long a skirt it will make.

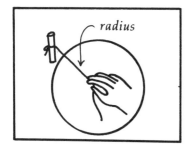

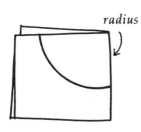

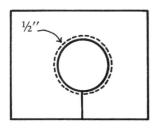

First you must find out what size circle will fit around your waist and what its radius is. If you are good at algebra, you can begin by measuring the circumference of your waist, and use the formula C (circumference) $= \pi 2r$ to discover the radius. If you prefer, you can find the radius with a simple compass made from a length of string and a piece of chalk.

Tie one end of the string around the piece of chalk, hold the other end of the string down firmly on a piece of paper, several inches away from the chalk, and scribe a circle with the chalk. The distance between the chalk and the center of the circle is the radius of the circle. If your waistline measures more than 20 but less than 30 inches, make a compass with a string that is 3½ inches long from chalk to end of string. Scribe a circle. Use a tape measure to measure around the circumference of the circle, and see how close the figure is to the circumference of your waistline. By lengthening or shortening the piece of string, make the circle either larger or smaller until it is the right size. Note the length of the radius on your Measurements Chart.

Use this radius to cut a sample waistline from scrap material. You need a piece of fabric about 15 inches square. Fold the material in quarters and use the point of the fold as the center of your circle. Scribe a quarter circle with the same radius as your waistline, and cut it out. Make a slit 5 inches deep on one side of the circle for a placket opening and try on the pattern. If it doesn't fit, make another one. When you have a pattern the correct size, make the circle ½ inch larger to allow for the placket seams by trimming the edge a small amount.

Now you need some skirt-length measurements. If

you have not already done so, measure from your waistline to the middle of your knee and write this number down on your Measurements Chart. Measure from your waistline to your ankle, and write that number down. Add the radius of your waistline to each figure in turn, and jot these totals down on a piece of paper.

Each of the final figures above—waistline radius plus skirt length—represents the total radius of the skirt. The sizes of round tablecloths are based on the diameter of the cloth. Since the radius of a circle is one half its diameter, a knee-length skirt that has a total radius of 30 inches can be made from a round tablecloth with a diameter of 60 inches. Get a tablecloth of exactly the right size, and you won't have to hem the entire outside of a full circle.

In addition to the tablecloth, you will also need enough extra fabric to finish the placket and the waistline. This material can be close to the tablecloth in color and weight, or you might like it to be a contrasting color, using it as trim and buying enough to make a pocket to match, thus tying the whole skirt together. You will also need a spool of matching thread and a hook and eye.

When you have found a tablecloth that suits you, fold it in quarters and scribe on it a quarter circle that has the same radius as your waistline, just as you did on the pattern. Cut the circle out $\frac{1}{4}$ inch inside the line to add seam allowance. Cut a slit 5 inches deep on one side of the circle for a placket opening. (It doesn't make any difference where you cut the slit, but the side with the slit automatically becomes the left-hand side of the skirt.) Try on the skirt and lengthen the placket if necessary.

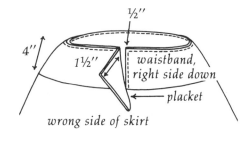

½"

4"   1½"   waistband,
              right side down

              ← placket

wrong side of skirt

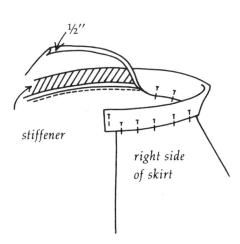

½"

stiffener

right side
of skirt

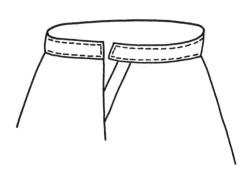

Finish the placket with a continuous lap placket, as described in Chapter 3. To make a **standard waistband,** cut a strip of material 4 inches wide and as long as the waistline of your skirt plus 2 inches. You need to stiffen the waistband, so it will better hold its shape, by putting a separate strip of heavier material, such as duck or canvas, inside the waistband. Cut the strip of heavy material 1 inch shorter and 1 inch narrower than the waistband. Sew the waistband to the skirt, right side of waistband to wrong side of skirt, with the end of the waistband at the back of the skirt extending 1½ inches past the placket opening, and with the end at the front extending ½ inch. (The long end of the waistband will lie under the short end when finished, to give a smooth appearance.) Turn the waistband to the front of the skirt, making a fold down the center. Place the extra strip of material inside the fold, with its top edge just touching the crease. Turn the raw edge of the waistband under, just over the first row of stitches, and pin the waistband to the skirt.

Fold the raw edges at each end of the waistband inside ½ inch and pin in place. Stitch the final seam of the waistband, including the two ends. Then make a row of stitches ⅛ inch below the top of the waistband to hold the facing securely in place.

Sew on the hook and eye at the waistband, and your tablecloth skirt is finished!

CIRCLE SKIRT FROM FABRIC

You don't have to use a round tablecloth to make a circle skirt, of course. You can cut the skirt from regular fabric. A full-length circle skirt is elegant for evening wear. You might make it of either a fairly stiff drapery material—a metallic tapestry fabric, for example—or a super-sheer voile or organdy. The latter might be a white skirt with a waistband covered with a blue velvet ribbon.

The skirt is made of two half circles, cut crosswise or lengthwise of the material. To estimate how much fabric you will need, you can scribe a pattern for the half circle on the floor, then measure the half circle and double the amount. You will, however, need a new waistline radius, since you must allow 2 inches for the side seams. Draw the new circle with a circumference that is 2 inches larger than your waist. To get this, begin by adding ¼ inch to the radius of your waistline and adjust the radius until it is right.

In the center of your floor space scribe a half circle with the new waistline radius. If possible, use the line of a floor board for the diameter or straight edge of the half circle. Add to this radius the desired length of the skirt plus ¾ inch, and scribe another half circle outside the first, basing your compass on the center point of the first half circle. Measure from this center point to the bottom of the skirt to find the necessary width of material. Measure the straight line at the top of the half circle and multiply the total by two to learn the necessary length of material to buy.

Before erasing the chalked pattern from the floor, use a tape measure to measure around the bottom of the skirt. Multiply this figure by two to find how much seam binding to buy. If you decide to make a skirt of fairly stiff drapery fabric, plan to finish the placket with seam binding, too, and add another 12 inches to the amount you are to buy. If your skirt is to

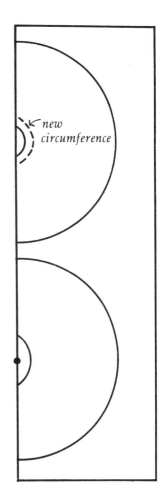

new
circumference

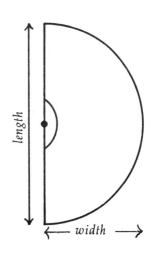

length

width

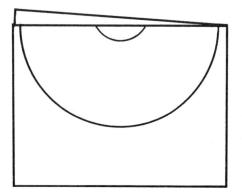

be made of a lighter, softer material, you can use leftover scraps to finish the placket. If the waistband is to be a standard waistband and made of the same material as the skirt, be sure to buy enough extra material for it. If the waistline is to be finished with an inside facing (see Chapter 6), it can be made of any strong flexible material. You will also need a spool of matching thread and a hook and eye.

When you are ready to cut out the skirt, if your material is lightweight, fold it in half crosswise or lengthwise, so that you can cut out both sections of the skirt at the same time. Scribe the two half circles according to the measurements you worked out. Pin the material together along the edges, to be sure the fabric is held straight as you cut.

Put the skirt halves together, right side to right side, and sew one side seam from top to bottom, making a ½-inch seam. Leave a placket opening the right length at the top of the second seam, and sew from that point to the bottom of the skirt. Finish the opening with a continuous lap placket (see Chapter 3), then apply the waistband.

Your skirt is now finished except for sewing on the hook and eye at the top of the placket opening and for hemming the bottom. Before doing the latter, fasten the waistband of the skirt to a clothes hanger hung in a doorway and let it stay there overnight, in case the material tends to pull out of shape from its own weight. The next morning, fold the skirt in quarters and check the bottom edge. If it is not exactly even, chalk around the bottom and trim off any excess below the chalk line. Turn up a ¾-inch hem and follow the directions for a standard hem with seam binding (see Chapter 4). Hemming the skirt will take

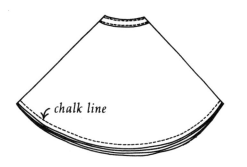

chalk line

quite a lot of time, but when you see what an elegant skirt you have made, you won't begrudge a moment of it.

WRAPAROUND SKIRT

There are three good reasons why one of the handiest skirts you can own is a wraparound. A wraparound skirt goes on very quickly; the double thickness of the lapped section of the skirt means that you don't have to wear a slip under it; and its waistband adapts to any temporary change in the size of your waist. Furthermore, it is one of the easiest garments in the world to make.

It is a good idea to cut a pattern for this skirt, since you will want to use it often, and cutting the right waistline requires some experimentation. The skirt is a half circle, and it can be any length you choose. The permanent pattern for it can be made of newspaper, but you will begin by making a pattern for the waistline out of a piece of scrap material 15 by 30 inches.

To make the two circle skirts, you needed a waistline that would fit you exactly, but for the wraparound you want the skirt to go around your waist 1½ times. Start with a compass radius that is three times longer than the radius of your waistline—the figure you wrote on your Measurements Chart. Scribe a half circle on one of the long sides of the material and cut it out. Discard the half circle and wrap the other piece of material around your waistline to see if it goes around your waist 1½ times. If the waistline is too small, make it larger by trimming ½ inch off the half circle. If it is too large, start again with a new piece of material and

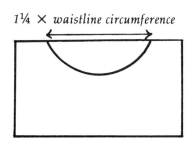

1¼ × waistline circumference

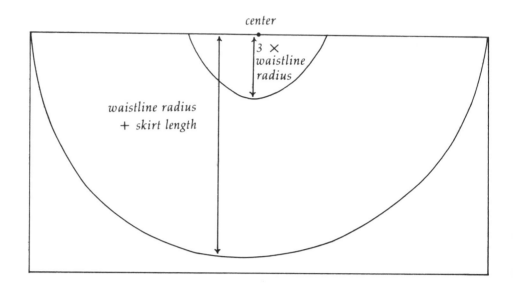

3 ×
*waistline
radius*

*waistline radius
+ skirt length*

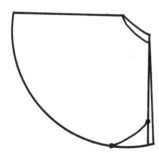

a smaller radius. Adjust it until you have a half circle the right size. Measure and mark down the length of the radius of the half circle. Measure from your natural waistline to the length you want the finished skirt to be, jot the figure down, and add it to the waistline radius. You need material this wide, and twice as long, to make the wraparound skirt.

Cut the skirt pattern out of taped-together newspaper. Use your pattern for the waistline to draw the first half circle, and with the compass at the same starting point, scribe another half circle below it with a radius that is the combined length of the waistline radius and the skirt length. Fold the pattern in half lengthwise (with the waistline at the top and the hem at the bottom) to make a quarter circle. The two sides of the half circle will be the opening of the skirt, and they should be rounded at the bottom, in the same way you rounded the bottom of the country shirt.

All edges of this skirt are finished with a narrow bias binding. The waistline is finished with a piece of the binding that is long enough to tie around your waist. Measure all the edges of the skirt except the waistline and jot down the total. Wrap a piece of string 1½ times around your waist, add 30 inches, and add this figure to the first one to see how much binding you will need. You hardly need to be told, at this point, that you can save money by cutting your own bias binding from material that contrasts with the skirt material.

The skirt should be made of a fabric heavy enough to hold its shape, such as duck, denim, or other similar sports material. The binding can be of any suitable wash-and-wear material that is soft and flexible enough to use as bias tape. Remember that 1 square foot of material makes about 8 feet of 1-inch-wide bias tape. You also need a spool of thread to match the binding.

Making the skirt is simplicity itself. Fold your material in half crosswise, and cut the skirt double using the pattern folded. Place the fold of the pattern on the fold of the material. Sew the binding to all edges of the skirt except the waistline, right side of binding to wrong side of skirt. Fold the binding over to the front, turn the raw edge under, and stitch in place.

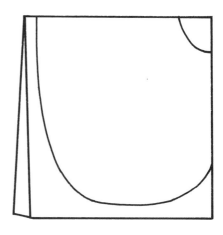

Lay the strip of binding for the waistline in place right side of binding to wrong side of skirt. Be sure that the binding extends 15 inches past both ends of the waistline. Sew it in place, then fold it over to the right side of the skirt and pin down. Fold the two long ends of the binding so that they match the folds of the binding that will be sewn to the waistline, and stitch along the entire length. Tie a small knot exactly at each end of the finished strip.

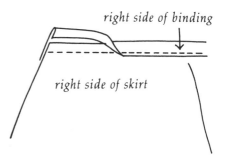

right side of binding

right side of skirt

Wrap the skirt around your waist, with the lapped section either in front or in back, tie the two ends of the binding together, and wear it. Would you have believed a skirt could be so easy to make?

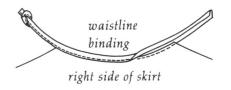

waistline binding

right side of skirt

· 10 ·

Instant Sweaters: A Pullover, a Cardigan, and a Vest

If you have ever knit a sweater by hand, you know how much yarn and how many hours of work it takes, and you know, too, how much store-bought sweaters cost.

If you've ever turned a commercially made sweater inside out, you may have noticed that some of them are not really knit in the traditional way, but are cut from fabric and sewn together. Since you can do this yourself, and since there are so many knit fabrics on the market today, why not make your own sweaters the way some factories do?

Knit fabrics can be used for a wide variety of garments, from underwear to overcoats, and because there are many different types of knits, it is a good idea to become familiar with them before deciding which ones to select. No one set of directions for handling knit fabrics applies to all of them, so you need to look over and learn how to handle the particular kinds you buy.

Some knits are thin synthetic jerseys so slippery that they require special techniques. There are also thin cotton or cotton-synthetic combinations that hold their shape better than the slippery kinds, and there are endless varieties of heavier knits that hold their shape well and can be sewn like any other material of the same weight.

Some knits, particularly the thin jerseys, cannot be sewn with a standard sewing-machine needle, but require a ball-point type. Since a ball-point needle can also be used for sewing other fabrics, you can, if you like, get one for your sewing machine and use it for everything.

Knit fabrics must be straightened before they are cut as they may be stretched out of shape when you buy them. If the knit you choose can be washed and dried by machine, simply put the fabric through the washer and drier cycles you will use for the finished garment. This will return the fabric to its proper shape. Some knits must be hand-washed, and if this is the case with the fabric you bought, hand-wash it to straighten it. If your knit is one of the rare ones that isn't washable, simply use the methods for straightening fabrics described in Chapter 1. (If you are not sure how your fabric is to be cleaned, cut a sample piece and test it for washability as described in Chapter 7.)

If you are using one of the thinner knits, you may find it advisable to pin the material to newspaper, using lots of pins to hold it in place, and cut each pattern piece with a matching backing of newspaper. Don't use fresh newspaper as the ink will rub off. Newspaper that is a week or more old is best. Sew the pattern pieces with the newspaper in place, then rip off the paper when you are finished.

The best thread for sewing all knit fabrics is a spun polyester, which has a certain amount of stretch in it. Most knits should be sewn with either a very narrow zigzag or with a long stitch (approximately 9 stitches to the inch). In the latter case, stretch the fabric slightly as you sew. When the fabric relaxes, you will have built stretch into your seam. Generally, either of these stitches is better than the so-called stretch stitch on the newer machines since the stretch stitch is too heavy and is difficult to remove to correct mistakes.

It is a good idea to experiment with your fabric before you begin work on an actual garment. All knit fabrics available on the market can be sewn on almost any machine, but you may need to try different techniques before arriving at those that are right for any particular knit and for your particular machine. Put two thicknesses of the material together and stitch a seam, then remove the material from the machine and take a look at it. Check the seam for strength. Some knits need to be sewn with double seams. If your knit does, be sure to stretch the fabric as you sew each seam.

Now look at the cut edges of your fabric and check for ravels or curled edges. If your fabric is prone to either of these, either sew all seams double as above or finish the edges with a zigzag stitch.

When you are thoroughly familiar with the fabric you are using, you are ready to go ahead and make yourself a few instant sweaters.

BATWING PULLOVER

You can begin with a classic sweater that fits comfortably and looks good with skirts, shorts, or slacks. The pattern is based on your Basic Blouse pattern (see Chapter 3).

Start with a full sheet of standard-size newspaper spread out flat. Fold in half your pattern for the front of the basic blouse and lay it out on the newspaper so that it runs up and down the long dimension of the paper, with the center line of the pattern on the left side of the newspaper. Start at the shoulder seam and with a ruler draw along it and extend it to the opposite, right-hand edge of the newspaper. Mark a point—A—8 inches below the end of this line on the same edge of the newspaper. This represents the bottom of the sleeve. Mark another point—B—3 inches above your natural waistline and a third point—C—8 inches below the waistline as shown. Chalk in the side seam of the new pattern between points B and C, and draw a horizontal line through point C for the new bottom of the pattern.

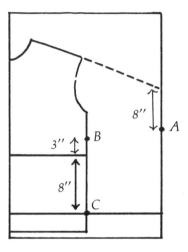

You are now ready to make the "batwing" of this particular pattern. Look at the drawing and join points A and B—you completely eliminate the armhole section of the original pattern and substitute the "batwing." Then use your pattern for an oval neckline (see Chapter 1) to draw the neckline on this pattern.

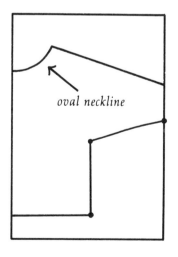

oval neckline

Cut out the pattern and make a sample garment from muslin or other pattern-cutting material. Since the front and the back of the pattern are identical, with the exception of the depth of the neckline, you can cut out the back without bothering to make a

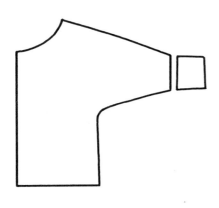

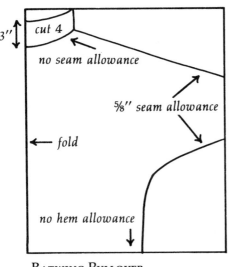

BATWING PULLOVER

separate pattern for it. Remember to add seam allowances at the neckline.

Using ⅝-inch seams, pin the front and the back together at the shoulders and down the sleeves, then pin the side seams. Slip it on and look at yourself in the mirror. If you want your finished sweater either longer or shorter, mark the exact amount of change needed at the bottom of the garment. In any case, remember to add 1½ inches for hem allowance when cutting the actual garment. When adjusting the side seams, remember to adjust both sides the same amount. If you want the sleeves shorter, mark them whatever length you decide upon, and if you want them longer, simply cut out extensions for them, following the shape of the present sleeves. Baste the extensions in place. If the neckline lies flat and goes on easily over your head, you do not need to change it.

The finished sweater will have a **turtleneck collar,** which does not need to be fitted. To cut the pattern for the collar, fold the pattern for the front of the batwing pullover in half lengthwise, and lay it on a piece of newspaper with the center line on the left-hand side of the newspaper and the neckline 3 inches below the top edge. Chalk around the neckline and remove the pattern. Draw a curve that exactly matches the neckline curve 3 inches above it. Connect the top and bottom of the collar with a vertical line at the right-hand edge.

This pattern is used for both the front and the back of the sweater collar, and also for the self-linings for the collar, so you will need to cut it out four times. Label the pieces.

With your pattern prepared, you are ready to buy

the fabric. Oddly enough, this sweater looks attractive in almost any weight of knit fabric, so you can make it to be worn either as a lightweight jersey or as a regular sweater.

Cut out the sweater. Then, because some knit fabrics have unique qualities that must be taken into consideration, baste the pieces together and try on the sweater. Not all but some knits require that the garment be cut smaller than your normal size if it is to fit well. If your basted sweater is too loose and sloppy, pin new seams to make it fit properly, and then trim accordingly.

The assembly of the sweater is simple and rather unusual. Fit the collar front to the sweater front, right side of collar to right side of sweater, and sew in place. Do the same to the collar back.

Match the front and the back of the sweater, right sides together, and pin the collar and shoulder seams. Pin the side seams, beginning at the underarm and pinning from there to the ends of the sleeves and the bottom of the sweater. Sew these seams.

Sew the lining pieces for the front and back of the collar together at the side seams to match the sweater collar. Lay the lining on the collar, right side of lining to right side of collar, and sew them together around the top edge. Turn the sweater wrong side out and fold the collar lining down over the collar. Pin in place, fold raw edge inside, and finish with invisible stitches. Hem the sleeve ends and the bottom of the sweater with standard hems (see Chapter 1), keeping your stitches loose to allow for stretch in the sweater material.

That's all there is to it.

Since this was your first venture with this pattern

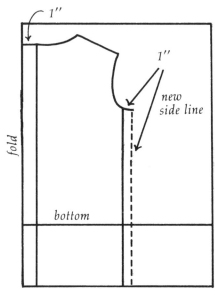

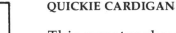

fold

bottom

new side line

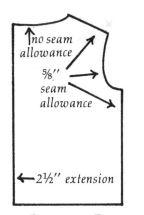

no seam allowance

⅝" *seam allowance*

←2½" *extension*

QUICKIE CARDIGAN, FRONT OR BACK

and with this type of garment, you almost certainly took longer to complete it than you will the next time you make it. With a little practice, you will understand why some people call this the "half-hour" sweater and make lots of them.

QUICKIE CARDIGAN

This sweater should be made of a medium-weight or heavyweight knit, and if you find one that is bonded, so much the better. (Bonded fabrics have a lining material laminated directly to the knit, which means that they are easy to sew and hold their shape perfectly.)

Use your Basic Shirt Dress pattern (see Chapter 8) as the basis for your cardigan pattern, and start with a sheet of newspaper, a yardstick, a tape measure, and a piece of chalk.

First measure the length that you want your cardigan to be, and mark a horizontal line across the paper that distance from the top. The Basic Shirt Dress pattern has an extra 1½ inches extending beyond each center front, but you will need 2½ inches on the cardigan for easy bound buttonholes. Lay the Shirt Dress pattern folded in half lengthwise on the newspaper with the center line 1 inch away from the left-hand edge. Chalk around the neckline, along the shoulder line, and around the armhole. Chalk a side seam 1 inch outside the present seam line and extend the armhole to meet this line. Cut out the pattern and label it. Copy the relevant markings from the Shirt Dress pattern, and also note the 2½-inch extensions to the front. To make a **fitted long sleeve,** lay the Basic Short-Sleeve pattern (see Chapter 8) on another piece of newspaper and chalk around the armhole. Refer to your Measurement Chart to find the length of your arm from shoulder to wrist and mark a point on the newspaper this distance from the top of the sleeve. Draw a horizontal line through this point. Now draw a vertical line to divide the sleeve in half and mark points on the bottom line 4½ inches away from it on each side. To make the side lines of the sleeve, use your ruler to draw lines from the bottom of the armhole to the points on the bottom line. Cut out the pattern and label it.

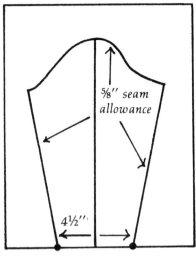

CARDIGAN, FITTED LONG SLEEVE

The back of the sweater pattern is cut exactly like the front, except for the neckline and the front extensions. Copy the pattern for a fitted neckline from the pattern for the back of the shirt dress.

The cardigan will button down the front, so you will need to buy buttons as well as a spool of matching thread for it. The buttons will be set 3 inches apart. Measure to find out how many you need.

Cut out the pattern pieces, remembering to add ½-inch seam allowance to the neckline.

Finish the front opening before assembling the rest of the sweater. The sweater front will be cut apart and sewn for easy bound buttonholes exactly as the tailored shirt was in Chapter 5. The only change is that instead of putting the hems in by machine, you may wish to put some of them in by hand with invisible stitches for a neater finish.

Now sew the shoulder seams, sew in the sleeves, and sew the side and sleeve seams. Easing in the sleeves is particularly simple with knits. To finish the neckline, if the sweater material is thin and flexible enough, cut a 1½-inch-wide bias strip from it, and use the strip to put a bias-binding inside facing around the neckline (see Chapter 3). Fold this strip under at the neckline of the sweater to avoid covering the buttonhole and the button set just below the neckline. Hem the sleeves and the bottom of the sweater by hand, and sew the buttons on the front.

If the material for your sweater is too thick to use for facing the neckline, you can bind the neckline as well as the ends of the sleeves and the bottom of the sweater with washable velvet ribbon, or with a bias binding cut from suede cloth. It is important to keep in mind, while you are sewing, that there is always a suitable technique for handling each different sort of material, so if one doesn't work or doesn't look right, just put on your thinking cap and figure out another way of doing it. Sometimes you will think of a method that makes the finished garment even more attractive than it would have been, so don't ever be afraid to use your imagination.

VEST OR WAISTCOAT

For hundreds of years the sleeveless garment known by one of these names has been a fashion favorite. It is both a comfortable and attractive kind of jacket; it adds warmth just where warmth is needed; and it can also be extremely decorative. The particular way in which a vest or waistcoat is cut changes from year to year, but the garment itself is always in style. In the Victorian period in England, waistcoats were worn mostly by men and were made from luxury materials heavily embroidered by sweethearts or wives. In Colonial America they were also worn by men but were often knee-length. Today they are worn by both men and women and can be any length you wish.

Basically a vest—we'll stick to that name for short—is a fitted sleeveless garment that is usually worn on top of a shirt, sweater, or whatever. To cut a pattern, begin with the Fitted Blouse with Darts pattern (see Chapter 5). The back and front of the vest pattern will be separately cut.

Get a sheet of newspaper large enough for the blouse pattern, fold the pattern for the back of the blouse in half lengthwise, and lay it on the paper. Make the new pattern 1 inch deeper at the armhole, as shown, and ½ inch wider at the side seam. Its length is 1 inch below the waistline marked on the blouse pattern. Copy the rest of the blouse pattern exactly.

Fold in half the front of the pattern for the basic blouse with darts, place it on another sheet of newspaper, and look at the drawing to see what changes must be made. They consist of enlarging the armhole, making the garment wider at the sides, changing the neckline to a deep slant, and making the point of the vest along the bottom edge.

Draw along the shoulder line, around the armhole, and down the side seam, changing the armhole exactly as you did on the back and making the side seam 1 inch wider. Mark a point 4 inches above your natural waistline on the left-hand side of the paper. Draw a line from the top of the shoulder line to this point. This is the new neckline. Draw a horizontal line 1 inch below the waistline. Measure the distance across the bottom of the pattern, from the center line to the side seam, divide the figure by three, and mark a point that is that distance from the center line and 4

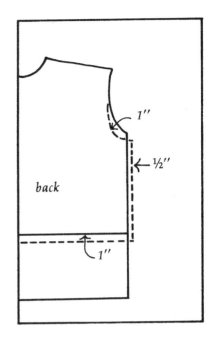

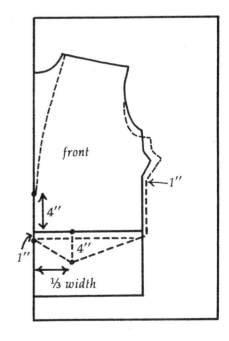

137

inches below the natural waistline. Draw a slanted line from the center line of the pattern, 1 inch below the waistline, to this point, and from there to the side seam, also 1 inch below the waistline. This makes the point at the bottom of the vest.

Cut out the back and front of the vest from pattern-cutting material. Pin the darts, side seams, and shoulder seams together, and try on the vest pattern. Check the fit. Note whether it is too long or too short, too tight or too loose, and make any necessary changes. Check the armhole to see if it is either too large or too small for your taste. If you would like to change it, you know how to do so. Mark and label the pattern.

It is easy to estimate how much material you will need, and it will be exciting to decide what type of material you wish to use. A vest is so ornamental that you can select a very vivid or unusual color or pattern to make yours especially interesting. You could, for example, select a striped or plaid knit, cut your vest on the exact bias of the material, and bind the edges with self-binding. Or you could select a sweater knit and bind all of the edges with suede cloth. Or you could get a riotously flowered fabric and bind it with washable velvet ribbon. (You could also cut a matching pattern to fit your boyfriend, and make a His and Hers set of vests.)

The vest itself is absurdly simple to make. Cut out the pattern pieces, stitch the side darts in the front, and sew together the shoulder seams. Sew the side seams, then bind all of the outside edges with whatever trimming you have chosen.

You have now completed all of the projects in this book, enlarging your wardrobe considerably and learning basic techniques you will use the rest of your life. Just because you have finished the book, however, doesn't mean that you are really through with it. If it has been successful, you are now ready to look back through the chapters and think of a dozen new projects to make. For example, you could make yourself a two-piece suit by combining the pattern for the vest with the pattern for the basic A-line skirt. You could make the vest and skirt of red velveteen and trim them with silver buttons. You could turn back to Chapter 9 and make a reversible wrap-around skirt completely lined with a contrasting material, make the tennis shirt in Chapter 3 of contrasting material, and be able to reverse the skirt for a mix-or-match outfit.

You could . . . , but there's no use making any further suggestions, because you yourself have already probably thought of many more. Have fun sewing!

Index

Duane Bradley grew up among women who, she reports, enjoyed sewing a great deal because they knew how to make exactly the clothes they wanted to wear out of whatever material they had on hand. Like Scarlett O'Hara, they could turn a pair of draperies into a ballgown or a pillowcase into an apron. Part of their method was to design their own patterns, which meant that the clothes fit properly and were becoming, and part of it was to use professional and commercial techniques for cutting and sewing.

Over the years, Miss Bradley has modified the procedures she learned as a child to suit new fabrics and new styles. The author of several books on sewing techniques, she has also written a number of children's books on other subjects.

Born in Clarinda, Iowa, she now lives in Henniker, New Hampshire, in a 150-year-old farmhouse.

Judith Hoffman Corwin is a book illustrator and a free-lance artist, many of whose assignments have involved stitchery or needlework. She brings to this book many years of experience with both the design and sewing of clothes.

A native of New York City and a graduate of Pratt Institute in Brooklyn, New York, she now lives in New York City with her husband and their son Oliver.